Searching for a
Silent God

— SARAH PARKINSON —

Sacristy
Press

Sacristy Press
PO Box 612, Durham, DH1 9HT

www.sacristy.co.uk

First published in 2019 by Sacristy Press, Durham

Sacristy Limited, registered in England & Wales, number 7565667

British Library Cataloguing-in-Publication Data
A catalogue record for the book is available from the British Library

ISBN 978-1-78959-038-8

For Richard, without whom this book would never have begun.

I wait for the Lord
more than watchmen wait for the morning,
more than watchmen wait for the morning.
Psalm 130:6 (NIV)

Foreword

In her investigative, intoxicating contemplation of paradox, *For The Time Being*, Pulitzer-Prize-winning author Annie Dillard sets off on an intuitive truth trail. A gumshoe mystic, she interrogates what she perceives to be "careless" and dark Divine anomalies, such as inexplicable, harrowing, human birth defects, whilst noting and cohabiting with the cryptic tensions of the Kabbalah, in which elusive and precise, esoteric Judaism affirms, *Out of that which is not/He made that which is.* "A planet sown in beings", as Annie Dillard sings, where swifts "mate in mid-air".

In *Searching for a Silent God*, the eventual, palatable unease of paradox—we are, for a season, in a mapless country here—preceded by the honest, moving search for the "lost narrative" of her relationship with God is the essence of Sarah Parkinson's engrossing, diligent and considerable testimony: a close-to-the-bone, open journal with poems, in which Sarah questions her first flush, "experiential" Christian conversion in the face of the stark, mortal removal of a greatly loved family member.

In conjunction with this bewildering, "fog-grey" loss comes the intensifying, cognitive development of Sarah's realization that the world's innumerable woes and inequities *cannot* be conveniently moved to another room because they're staining the hassocks of the tame and tidy sanctuary. The hermeneutical counsel to such questioning goes something along the lines of—best not to dwell too much on the glaringly insoluble, you'll only upset yourself.

The core of *Searching for a Silent God* is what the Franciscan philosopher, Richard Rohr, describes in his writings as the "evolution of consciousness", in which Sarah's acute and heartfelt poems are essential signposts for the reader; meditative stops along the path. A collective, pensive, slow-functioning compass, which doesn't always clearly indicate what the next direction could possibly be.

And while Sarah does not shrink from describing the cold abandonment she experiences of a God seemingly disappeared, with the accompanying gnawing sense of absence that that entails, the book becomes an absorbing pilgrim's paean to reframing and reimagining her soul's first and lasting Love. That ardour embracing a new understanding of the profound, sufficient, transcendental paradox and intimate conundrum of Jesus, who miraculously manifests the "deep magic" unity of the Trinity. The wilderness Saviour, once dependent on Mary's sustaining breast. God's first-born paradox, both human and Divine, personified thoroughly and sacrificially as the incarnational "jewel of the poor", the beleaguered and the desolate.

Searching for a Silent God is a restorative helpmeet for the faint-hearted and fearful, and a comforting companion for those who dare to hope that these "shadowlands" are but a temporary gloaming and travail. A brief suspense before the jaunts and jubilee to come.

Stewart Henderson
Poet, lyricist and broadcaster

Contents

Prologue

Absence

In some ways,
being close to you was like cavorting
across endless aeons with my lover.
You knew every curve and crevice
of my body,
every thought, and half-thought, and un-thought,
and space between thoughts
in my mind;
every catch of my breath, and all the gamut
of my emotions.
I took delight in the gradual discovery
of how much you knew,
and in discovering, uncovered more of you.
Then a moment came that I was
anticipating—
flashed like lightning across the sky of my experience,
seared a landscape of loss into my future.
And in death's grey-fog aftermath,
when I was too numb to know if you were near,
that was when you chose to disappear.
There is purpose in everything you do,
they say,
but every time I prayed into the bruised void
my words bounced off infinity,
and echoed only back to me.
And as if it weren't enough for you to walk away—

you had to steal the very substance
of the person I knew how to be.
I tried to tell myself it wasn't true,
and one day soon we'd meet again,
and I would understand the part you'd played
in midwifing my pain.
But hope went stale, and reason fled
as anger came to share my bed.
And now I understand the full extent
of what you've done, I wonder
who on earth I will become.

When a person loses their sense of connection with God, it seems that there are very few places to turn for reassurance or relief. There are not many modern resources that discuss this particular feature of relationship with God, although there are numerous stories in the Bible about God being silent. It is for this reason that I considered making my own story public, in the hope that it might be a refuge for anyone else who suffers through the kind of separation from God that I have done.

The poem above was my psalm of lament, a cry of sorrow and despair that reflected the bleakest time I have ever known in my walk with God. A relationship built on the cornerstone of Jesus' incredible gift of death and resurrection, that had spanned eighteen years, replete with joy and textured with trial, suddenly appeared to be severed as neatly as a hot wire cuts through polystyrene.

The circumstances around that severing were painful enough in themselves. My mother-in-law, Margaret, was diagnosed with pancreatic cancer in May 2012, a point at which my husband, Richard, and I did not live near her, though we had in the past. She was given three to six months to live. Naturally there was Richard's shock and grief to anticipate and support. I had also built up a strong affection for Margaret during the early years of my marriage, when we had been able to spend a great deal of time together. I knew, therefore, that I would also have my own grief to work through, as well as a young family to sustain throughout the hammer blows of the next few months.

Now, I am well aware that we were not the first family to suffer from such a horrific shock, and nor will we be the last. But in this story of mine, this story about the absence of God, the experience of Margaret's death in September 2012 appears to be pivotal. I remember so well how, during those few short months of horrified anticipation, I felt as though I was taking a long, slow breath. It was as though I was breathing God in, in defence against the wound that was to come. My trust in God, that he would be my guide and my strength as I attempted to support Richard and confront my own grief, was absolute.

My experience of the following six months—one that my own anecdotal evidence suggests is shared with others who are bereaved—was that of grey numbness, a lack of feeling or sense. The weight of it seemed to drag my eyes to the ground, leaving me unable to look up and see the faces of those who grieved with me. I could feel neither anger, nor passion, nor frustration, nor empathy, nor compassion. All that kept me moving forwards was the sure knowledge that God had always been with me, for as long as I had asked him to be, and that when my self woke up again at some unspecified point in the future, I would know his love and courage and strength again.

My "reawakening" took place around six months after Margaret's death. I well remember the almost physical sensation of finally being able to lift my eyes off the ground and look around me again. I finally dared to allow empathy to re-enter, and to consider how much pain Richard was carrying. It took a little time—I can't remember how long—for me to realize that the sense of God's presence, which I had known since the day of my conversion in my early twenties, was no longer a part of my life. Not even the occasional light of a distant communication was left, and prayer had about the same effect as shouting into an echo chamber. Bluntly speaking, God was blanking me: neither saying anything to me, nor receiving anything I tried to say to him. He had withdrawn himself from me, and was stubbornly refusing to return.

To reassure any who are now reaching for their Bibles to find the many, many verses that prove such a statement false, there has never been a time when I have not known the *fact* of God's presence with me. I have found this paradox incredibly difficult to explain when trying to describe my situation: that on the one hand there is a truth I know, that God is always with me; but on the other hand, my experience of what could be described as spiritual sensory deprivation has rendered it impossible to live within that truth.

This book is about my slow and painful progress towards reconciling the gap between the two ends of the paradox: it is my (hopefully) honest attempt to make a record of that process, and I began it when I was in the very darkest part of my journey, which was marked by many kinds of loss, all woven together with my anger at being so fully abandoned by the person I had relied upon to help me through my grief.

The first half of the book is about my life in faith before this time of absence began, which I hope will enable the reader to build up a sufficient picture of my relationship with God and how it developed during that period. This, I hope, will set the context for the second half, which deals with my journey through recognizing and processing the sense of his absence. In order to try and convey my experience as fully as possible, I have made no attempt to excuse or justify it. I simply set it before the reader as clearly and openly as I can, as a testimony to where I was then, and where I am travelling to now. If my story holds up a mirror to yours, and you find some relief in knowing that you are not alone, then this book has served the purpose for which it was intended, and I am deeply glad.

Part 1: Presence

Chapter 1

A good place to alight upon this story might be my experience of living with a parent who, when I was in my early teens, decided to turn to God out of a deep spiritual need for solace (in my view at the time, rather obnoxiously). Naturally I could only roll my eyes and tease my mother about it, arguing theology with her occasionally in much the same way as I would my Religious Education teacher at school. Essentially this entailed mocking her beliefs and stating each of my own studiously agnostic opinions as fact, as you would expect any high-spirited fourteen-year-old to do. Her conversion experience, however, likely had a greater impact on me than I could have guessed at the time. Certainly her story of "finding God" made a distinct impression on me, resulting as it apparently did from the faithful prayers of a child in the class she taught at school, and a rather significant dream she had about Jesus, who showed her the wounds in his hands. Raised up to that point in a secular home, such language was wildly outside of my own experience. I set it aside for the time, however, enduring my mother's new-found fervour and church activities as best I could, and teasing her about it whenever I saw fit.

I followed the usual course of education that those gifted with enough memory to pass exams usually take: GCSEs, A Levels and then university. I chose psychology for my undergraduate studies, reflecting my curiosity about the inner workings of the human mind.

I was two years into my university course when God wedged his foot in the door far enough that I couldn't close it again. My mother, divorced and raising my brother and me alone since we were young children, met someone and fell in love. We lived in Germany at the time, as she was a primary school teacher for the Armed Forces, but he lived in England. She decided, then, to move back to England and spend more time with him, thinking that it could be serious, and soon after she moved they decided to get married.

The short space of time in which this happened meant that I had not had time to get to know the place my mother had moved to. She therefore very thoughtfully arranged for members of her new church to "keep an eye" on me while she and my new stepfather were away on honeymoon. To be brutally honest, the thought of this filled me with far more dread than the thought of spending two whole weeks on my own. I have never been uncomfortable with solitude, and quite relished the thought of it: my social awkwardness made me feel wary about having to spend time with people that I knew very little about, particularly those who might show an over-keen interest in my spiritual wellbeing.

I had every reason to be wary. Somehow, these people offered me company, friendship and kindness, and managed to create a space in which I suddenly began to feel very curious about God and faith. Somehow, it felt safe enough to ask the questions that began to press in on me, and by the end of the first week I was ready to talk to the Big Yin myself. I was very aware that, certainly in the church culture I was falling in with, it was common for such things to happen with another person of faith alongside you. It was practically expected. Stubborn and private as I am, though, this particular conversation was only going to happen one way: in solitude, in my mother's house, with words of my own choosing that didn't follow any particular recommended formula. This was as much because I didn't know what might come of my first conversation with so-called God as it was because I wanted to feel comfortable enough to say whatever came to me.

The actual "moment", as it were, might be considered as something of an anti-climax, especially to those who look for excitement and glamour in the movement of God's Spirit through the world. As a matter of fact, I finally began to address God directly when I was mopping the kitchen floor. Somehow this practical, methodical task helped to clear my thoughts to express what seemed to be pulling me in his direction, along with all the doubts and questions and worries I had about the whole experience. I said no words of absolute confidence and faith. To paraphrase, since I have no power to remember such detail, my offering to God was something along the lines of: "Well, I'm not sure if you're real or not, but just in case you are let's give it a go."

A more equivocal conversion prayer you could not ask for, I am sure. Yet, to my shock and surprise, it was as though God shrugged his shoulders and said, "OK, that's good enough for me." I kid you not. And from that day it was as though someone had lit a fire inside me, and I could not do enough to discover what this new life of faith meant for me. I prayed, I read, I learned worship songs on the guitar, I studied, I got baptized. I took this passion back to university for my final year, joined the Christian Union, found a church, and began to consider what impact this new faith might have on the decisions I had to make about the next step after university. And thus began the journey towards a place that would significantly shape the course of the rest of my life.

◆   ◆   ◆

Whilst at university it was a source of some regret for me that I had not taken a year out before beginning my degree. I knew myself well enough to recognize that this was largely due to my innate preference for taking the easiest route—and a continuation of a life of study was definitely more appealing to me than taking on a minimum-wage job and living with my mother. But the thought of taking some time out after graduation still hung in the air, and so I consulted my church leaders about the possibility of volunteering to do some overseas work for a Christian mission organization. I was surprised when the response came back: "Have you considered going to Bible College?" Of course I hadn't! The time ought to have been over for reading books and writing essays, but the idea gripped me and wouldn't let go. The prospect of having a thorough grounding in theology and good training in offering Christian ministry was arresting, though the issue of how it was to be paid for was another matter entirely.

I was still young enough to pursue such an idea because it felt like "the right thing to do", though even then I did not have the temerity to declare that God wanted me to do it. I was, however, possessed of a kind of fatalistic assumption that all would be well, that I didn't need to dig any deeper into my motives, and that somehow the practical arrangements would simply fall into place. These days, I tend to experience a strange mixture of remorse at my youthful assumptions and gratitude to my mother, who ended up supporting me financially.

In hindsight, and knowing more about myself now, I am aware that the drive to continue in education came at least partly from my own preference for study over work (as any member of my family will agree immediately with a sigh and a roll of their eyes). I am also aware now, though, of my need to have as much information as possible before making a decision. Since the question of what to do with the rest of my life was such a huge one, and I wanted very much to keep God at the centre of any future path I chose to take, it felt appropriate in a very logical way.

In due course I applied to two different Bible Colleges, Redcliffe College in England and Belfast Bible College in Northern Ireland, and was accepted at both. What followed was a decision-making process that, I believe, was an early indicator of how my understanding about the way God works with me to make such choices would be shaped.

I was largely surrounded by a theology that emphasized God's plan over and above free will. Yes, there was intellectual assent amongst my fellow churchgoers to the need to balance both concepts. In practice, however, the overriding assumption seemed to be that when there was a big decision to be made, God would clearly point the way out to the faithful person. However, I could not honestly say to myself or anyone else that I believed God was showing me what to do: all I knew was that I had long held a secret, romantic desire to "discover" Ireland. I was concerned, as I didn't want that desire to colour how I made the decision about where to study, if it meant disobeying God. It took a great deal of prayer and wrestling with my thoughts to come to the conclusion that, actually, God didn't mind where I went, but cared far more about how I conducted myself whilst there. It struck me that since God had made me who I was, secret romantic desire to go to Ireland and all, perhaps it would actually be all right to just go. Especially since there was no major difference between the two courses I had applied for. And so off I went.

◆   ◆   ◆

During my interview for admission to the college, the main concern that had been expressed by the interview panel was my relative inexperience in terms of Christian knowledge and growth. I was happy to agree, given that I had been following Jesus for little more than a year when I started my two-year course, in the autumn of 1997. I was determined to give no cause for concern, therefore, and to conduct myself in a manner worthy of what I felt to be a generous trust in my calling and abilities. Although the college had had fairly restrictive rules in the past, only one specific requirement remained that I felt could have a bearing on me, and I was determined to abide by it at any cost. I had become fed up with men and dating anyway, so an admonition to avoid entering any relationships with other students in one's first term at college seemed fairly easy to abide by.

And so, naturally, it transpired that I ended up becoming engaged to another student at the college within three months of arriving there.

The particulars are a little messy to go into, especially since (notwithstanding my avowed distaste for dating) I had met a young man in England shortly before leaving for college, who, not long after I moved to Belfast, rang me to declare passionately, "God has told me that we're going to get married." Perhaps my experience with choosing which college to go to had already taught me something about such declarations, because the best response I could come up with was, "Well, it's a bit early to tell, isn't it?" All these years later I can look back and reflect on how foolish I was to form an attachment to someone I had known for so short a time when I was about to move away, and I can see how doing so might have resulted from a sense of vulnerability in going somewhere unfamiliar.

One fringe benefit of this folly was that, considering myself attached to one young man, I was able to form a friendship with the man who *would* become my husband, free from any expectations of that friendship becoming anything more serious. So there was perhaps some good to come out of my naïveté, in that it enabled me to build a strong foundation for the relationship that would shape the rest of my life.

◆   ◆   ◆

Aside from such momentous decisions as who to marry, those two years at college were a time in which I absorbed a vast amount of information about the Bible and the Church. I began as well, perhaps most significantly, the process of learning to address questions of theology and doctrine without necessarily having to find answers. I was fortunate enough to be taught doctrine by the inestimable Drew Gibson, who preferred to present us with a range of options on each topic, from which he left us to draw our own conclusions. I am grateful to this day for his method, which taught me that taking answers that are spoon-fed has nothing like the power of wrestling with the questions oneself: to do so with openness and honesty is one of the great keys to learning more about ourselves and God.

From the beginning of my conscious relationship with God, I had been as open and honest as I knew how to be with him, so perhaps I was particularly suited to receiving this style of teaching well. It did not mean I didn't struggle; when it came to prayer I had questions that for a long time seemed to have no answer, and although I wanted to submit to what I believed to be right, I was too restless and spiritually sore to do so fully.

It is quite remarkable how a person with no church background and only a few months' experience of faith can fall prey to "what makes a good Christian", or "what makes a person's faith in Jesus valid". And so, in my early days, eager to do all I could to prove to God and myself that this relationship was the most important thing in my life, I followed every piece of advice that my largely conservative church leaders taught me. The "quiet time" was a centrepiece of faith: a space in the day in which you were to read your Bible, study it and pray for the things that God prompted you to pray for. Although I probably could not have put words around it at the time, the understanding I received was that if you weren't engaging in your quiet time, you were very likely backsliding and could possibly lose your faith.

I look at the quiet time now with a faint horror at the limitations it places on the possibilities of prayer, but also with an understanding of how the structure and discipline of it can be useful at certain points in our journey towards God. Again, although not consciously measuring it at the time, I suspect I felt the quiet time ranked higher than either the moments I spent in unstructured, conversational prayer with God or the time I spent journaling about my relationship with him. But then, about half way through my time at the college, my quiet times began to feel like more of a prison than a liberation. When I became aware of this change, I found that my desire for meaningful interaction with

God struggled against my obedience to what I believed was his intention for my prayer life.

Looking back, I cannot remember how I began to understand the difference between the imposed expectations of other people and the life-giving relationship that God wanted me to experience with him. I believe it took many months after I gave up a daily quiet time for me to stop feeling the heavy burden of guilt that I had dragged along behind me so unnecessarily all that time. But eventually I began to understand better the value of unstructured, unlimited prayer, and of exploring faith through my writing—both prose and poetry. These dealt with the rough edges of life, where doctrine rubbed up against reality and forced me to try and make sense of difficult and complex things.

The two years I spent in college were instrumental in laying a foundation for a faith that was not locked down into reliance on a set of beliefs, but that opened me up to seeing God at work in a broken, messy world, and discovering my own part in it.

◆   ◆   ◆

Although I often feign embarrassment when telling the story of how I met Richard, I must confess to a secret pride in the dispatch with which we went from establishing our friendship to promising to spend the rest of our lives together. The worst part, of course, was the knowledge that I was directly disobeying the college's rule about not entering into any romantic relationship during my first term there. So with a nod of apology to Belfast Bible College, I hereby confess that we were dating within three weeks of the beginning of term one (the other poor chap didn't stand a chance, really), and were engaged before the end of that November. Yes, I met and became engaged to my future husband within less than three months. Fortunately, it turned out not to be such a foolish move as you might expect from so young a couple. And the benefit, of course, was that it gave us the greatest part of the two years I was there to think and plan for and pray about our future.

The question of purpose is a deep and pervading one, and one that, if we don't ask it, commits our lives to mediocrity and dullness. However, to ask it is an immensely daunting task, and we may well never find a complete answer. Nevertheless as a couple we asked it, because we were young and inexperienced, and full of fervour to serve God wherever it felt we could be of best use to him. Richard confessed at that time to a feeling that he might possibly be called to church ministry in some form; he didn't have full confidence in that calling, however, and was worried that the desire to lead a church might come more from his ego than from God calling him. And so we set that thought aside for a time, willing to return to it in the future if necessary. In the meantime, our conversation turned to the possibility of missionary work.

Our college naturally provided information about opportunities after graduation, and in the course of time we came across a missionary organization offering work in a location that appealed to us. It required us to fundraise our own income and to submit to behavioural restrictions that our own, more liberal theology did not preclude from a life of faith. We were glad, though, to agree to both requirements in order to do the work we felt that God wanted us to do. We graduated in 1999, got married that summer, took temporary jobs in Belfast and began the task of raising money to support us in that work.

The mission project that we signed up for was not one that required us to move to a particularly exotic place, but it was nevertheless a place both Richard and I felt to be in great need of the work offered. We were to go to rural Ireland, to an island off the West Coast that nonetheless hosted a good handful of churches of different denominations. The work was to support these under-resourced places of worship, and it seemed to suit our talents and abilities quite well. The hard part was persuading sufficient people to agree with us enough on the need for the work to make the regular financial donations that would enable us to do it. We visited churches, raised awareness of the mission organization and of the project we were to become involved in, but found that enthusiasm for it was difficult to muster. We were of course aware that there would be some caution among Northern Irish Protestants about funding work in the South, and that may have been the greatest factor in our lack of success. To begin with, at any rate.

A year after our marriage I came across a job opportunity that appealed to me a great deal. Firstly, it was a temporary contract, only six months, so it wouldn't tie me down when it was time to leave for the South. Secondly, it paid a significant amount more than the oh-so-glamorous job I already had, working in the typing pool of an old-fashioned insurance firm. Thirdly, the work itself sounded fascinating, as did the organization advertising the job. With my fondness for all things academic, the prospect of being a research assistant was exciting: the organization was named Evangelical Contribution on Northern Ireland (or ECONI for short) and billed itself as a peace and reconciliation charity. Feeling oddly compelled, I applied for the job and was successful. It put Richard and me in a somewhat precarious position financially if we weren't ready to go to Ireland by the end of the contract, but we both hoped it would provide us with the motivation to work harder to be ready within that time.

I began working at ECONI in October 2000, and I think that this was perhaps one of the most transformative experiences of my life. The work largely consisted of typing up recorded interviews for the researcher, and preparing the text of her completed book for publication. In the process I listened to a wide range of evangelical women's views on the Church, faith and feminism, which in itself was a mind-broadening experience. However, much greater than the impact of the work I did was the distinctly profound influence the other members of staff had on me. ECONI was one of a group of third-sector peace-making organizations to whom the task fell to create a social and political atmosphere in which peace agreements could be reached within a deeply fractured society. It required people of great wisdom and spiritual maturity, of which there were several at ECONI.

Chapter 2

Faith crisis

Voracious in its appetite
it stalks.
A sleek-bodied
powerhouse of suffocating strength,
silent and inexorable.
Never confronting,
evading even peripheral vision.
Aim to grasp the substance
and my hand clutches
at shadow.
So insubstantial,
with what weapons
can it be destroyed?
With reason, and logic?
But these do not answer
to my yearning, burning
search for truth.
My constant shadow,
an unseen presence over my shoulder,
paints a black cloud around me
shielding what I seek.
The choice I thought was made,
the One I thought to be my reality:
is he there?

I cannot find you, and so
I plead with you,
I beg you
to find me.

Working with people who exhibited the faith and intuition required in the field of peace and reconciliation did create some difficulties for me. For starters, a random conversation could quite simply take the top of my head off and send my thoughts racing down paths of possibility I hadn't dared to allow myself to think of before. Questions that had been tugging at my elbow, perhaps almost since my conversion, but that I had suppressed out of concern that God wouldn't like them. God, not liking my questions? The thought sounds preposterous now, but I have already observed how quickly a "young" Christian can fall prey to misapprehensions about God, if that is how they are taught. I began to find my intellectual self engaging much more directly with my faith, in turn opening myself up to wider possibilities of God at work in the world, and in me. Over time I found a wildness and an exhilaration in my prayer life, an adventure that had been waiting to happen since perhaps before I was born.

This was the first difficulty. The second one was much, much more painful and heart-breaking to deal with. In the process of discovering this intellectual freedom in Christ, I found myself questioning every pillar of support upon which my faith had been built. Questions open a person up to uncertainty, and I began to be less and less sure of what was necessary and true about my faith. Bang! Down fell the unthinking reverence I used to have for scripture. Crash! There went the necessity to express my faith through works. I could sit on my hands for the rest of my life and still be loved by God. Loudest of all was the thunder resonating in my ears when I realized what a limited and narrow view of God I had so far learned from the Church. This God had cared more about my church attendance than about my compassion; he was more concerned with policing my theology (never put a thought out of line!) than with nurturing compassion. Pretty much everything I had been taught that a "good Christian" should do—Bible study, intercessory prayer, church attendance, tithing, you name it—all came crashing down about my ears, and I still remember one day, sitting on the sofa at home, when it felt that everything that had made my faith, that had connected me to God, was rubble at my feet.

It would be difficult to find the words to express the panic I felt clawing at my chest, the sense that everything was drawing in on me, and there was no way of breaking out of the enveloping blackness. But in a moment of unplanned prayer, desperate and desolate, in the very centre of that darkness, I asked the question: "All this is gone, Lord, but are you still here?"

I have never been able to claim that I have heard God speak words to me in the same way as if another human said them. It has taken me many years to develop a degree of confidence in my ability to discern what God wants to tell me: back then it was incredibly rare for me to be sure of what he wanted to convey. But this was one of those rarities. It was very, very faint—no doubt masked by the weight of my own doubts—but out of the darkness came the "yes" that I had been longing for.

Perhaps it was foolish of me not to recognize that within that harrowing experience, most if not all of my pain was the result of my innate desire for God. However, it was a foolishness that made no odds to God. He knew what I needed in order to cling on to him, and offered it to me freely. All I needed was him, stripped of every extraneous measure by which I was used to judging faith. The simple power of his love carried me out of that darkness, and we slowly began the process of building a relationship that didn't rely so much on rules as on grace and conversation. Over a long period of time, I even began to return to some of those "broken pillars" of my old faith, and understand their purpose better in this new, more liberated context.

While this inner tumult was ongoing, there were external influences on the missionary work my husband and I were preparing for. We did try to see the good in this, but we struggled a great deal to come to terms with it. New regional leaders came in, making drastic changes to the work we were to do. Instead of the country, the project was moving to the city. Instead of supporting under-resourced churches, we were to establish a new church in Dublin and a theological college. Relationships that had been built up in preparation, the visits we had made to the rural community, the vision for a work already in the making—all these were cast aside. This, along with my own new-found hunger for intellectual freedom in my faith, and questions Richard had that differed somewhat to my own, but tended towards the same conclusion, led us to decide that this project was not the best thing for us to take on after all.

It was an enormously difficult decision to make, perhaps because it felt in some ways like failure, despite a great deal of the events being out of our hands. It was very difficult to tell the mission staff who had worked with us for well over a year, as it felt as though we were letting them down. It was hard to tell our family and friends, particularly those who had already pledged to support us financially, and in some cases already begun their donations. Despite believing that we were doing the right thing, I am sure our pride was dented, and we were left with the not-very-unremarkable question of what on Earth we were supposed to do next. Fortunately, I was offered a new, longer-term post at ECONI after the research assistant role ended, so we did not have to make that decision in a great hurry.

Part of the pain of deciding not to continue with our missionary work was that it left us with a black hole of a question, a void within us that we were keen—perhaps even desperate—to fill. That question, of course, was: "If not this, then what?" Though in fairness, that question was the external expression of a much deeper question, one that drove to the very root of us to interrogate not just who we were, but also what our purpose was. For both of us, in different ways, the experience had shaken the foundations not just of our faith but of our sense of identity, and to live with such deep uncertainty about all things was extremely difficult. No wonder we were so keen to have these questions answered as soon as possible. We were looking for some sort of stability. However, we also recognized that we had been too hasty in deciding on our first career choice, so we decided not to rush into any alternative. We would remain where we were and spend some time learning how to listen to God, so that we could better discern what he wanted from us.

We carried on working in our respective jobs, and I continued to allow my new-found intellectual freedom to work itself into my faith, into God, and into me. I developed a passion for God's justice: a justice rooted in compassion and love. A justice that sought to provide the opportunity for every human being to live in peace and safety, and to discover and live out their purpose without fear.

◆   ◆   ◆

What then?

What then? She softly breathes
the question holding all her dreams.
What if? The stray and
gathering thought held tightly at the seam
of consciousness.
Scattered within hope and hurt
and treasured melodies,
the liquid beauty of the future's
undecided eulogy
arrests her choice.
And bow to bonds that shape her,
touching life within her hands;

a tender pain at parting,
though love might understand
her wakened need.
And take a path in faith and fear
that aches with potent need;
to serve, and trust, and know the power
of perfect place, and lead
the homeless home.
Frail as the slender stem of grass
beneath the harrowing sky,
yet uncalled strength in need may urge
the choice, despite her alibis,
and lead her home.

I felt it was breathtaking, how little I had learned through church teaching about my responsibility to actively care for the Earth and its people. It became imperative to me, a central driving force of my life in God. I developed a hunger for more knowledge of global justice, of poverty abroad and at home, and what potential there might be to eradicate it. I wondered aloud to Richard about ways to learn more, and that out-loud wondering turned into a quest to go back to university and study for a Master's degree in Social Development.

It was crazy, yes. In terms of career decision-making, perhaps the oddest move I could have made. It was financially costly, would land us in more debt, and—it turned out—would require us to uproot and move across the water, separating us from family, friends and workplace connections. We saw it then as the greatest act of trust in God we had ever made, separately or together. So, being young enough to be more full of possibility and hope than of risk and fear, in 2002 we packed up all our belongings into a Luton van and ferried ourselves across the Irish Sea, to eventually arrive in Swansea, on the South Coast of Wales.

When we had originally made the decision to move to Swansea, we had known no-one and nothing there at all. But by a strange serendipity my father had met a woman who lived there and decided to move to be with her about six months before we arrived. So we weren't completely alone after all, but we had no connections to Christian groups or churches in the area. Since making the decision to move away from missionary work, and in the wake of those roaring, tumultuous questions that had so dramatically reshaped my faith, I had wanted nothing more than to run away from the Church. I was aching and bruised and desolate and resentful and very, very angry that the institution I had trusted so completely had failed me, as I saw it then, so deeply. I needed time to heal, to discover the possibilities of God without intermediary or distraction and to learn (though then it was only a very faint thought) to one day be able to forgive.

Out of a sense of duty and obedience we did attend a few different local churches to see if that might be the better path for us to take. Two of the three were welcoming, but for myself I felt completely unable to interact with God within the confines of a service. Eventually we discovered a local Christian community that suited us a little better. The meetings were far less formal than those of a church congregation, so we started to go along. They took place in a pub and were attended by people who would have struggled to fit into the conventional kind of congregation we were used to. We were able to be open and honest about our circumstances with Sean, who organized and led the gatherings, and felt that among these people we could relax. Here, we weren't alone in experiencing a desire for God alongside an inability to comply with the expectations of a traditional congregation.

Richard and I fully believed that our decision to move to Swansea was part of our discipleship. It was a necessary step in the journey of discovering ourselves in order to discover how we should serve God. However, this belief was tested almost to breaking point within the first three months of arriving. We had savings and loans enough to survive for that period, and we were confident that Richard could find full-time employment within that time. To begin with, at least. By the end of November we were beginning to feel the first flutters of panic, and by mid-December we began to talk seriously about what we would do if we could no longer afford to stay in Swansea. We prayed together and separately for wisdom and faith, still sure that God wanted us to work out our calling, but becoming less sure that we were in the right place to do it.

At the very last possible point, or so it felt, Richard was offered a job that seemed ideal. At the time we saw this as a valuable lesson in trust, and our huge relief translated into gratitude to God. We viewed the job as his gift and as an affirmation that we were on the right track. I expect I would see things differently now, in the light of lived experience of the immortal truth expressed in the movie *Forrest Gump*, that in the end, "stuff" just happens. However, I still recall how fully and completely we felt we had to submit ourselves to God and whatever circumstances might follow, and I wonder whether it is something I could manage today.

◆   ◆   ◆

I studied at the University of Wales in Swansea, amongst a very diverse cohort of students, most of whom were already involved in social development. The experience afforded me a thorough grounding in the social, political and economic causes of poverty, and a much more realistic look at its effects than one might come across in the media or through charitable organizations. My studies enabled me to piece together a much broader and deeper understanding of the global balance of power than I had before, and of the fundamental injustices wrought by the misapplication and abuse of that power. With my background in peace-building at ECONI, I was particularly interested in looking at development in the context of conflict, and for my dissertation I studied the Israeli–Palestinian conflict in some depth.

I also had to complete a placement as part of my course, and I took this as an opportunity to discover more about social development in the UK. I was assigned to a community project in Swansea that was attached to a local independent church. It happened to be one that I had already attended once or twice with Richard, and had decided not to attend regularly. Engaging with a church in this practical way, however, I found to be a helpful exercise. It became a place where my faith-inspired learning choice met with the practical outworking of the gospel through God's people. That practical, caring action and the struggle for justice for those on the margins of society were to be key features in this next stage of my faith journey. I was firmly in a place where, if I wasn't showing love in action for the kinds of people that Jesus showed the most practical love for, I wasn't living the fullest expression possible of my faith.

I finished all my studies within the first twelve months of my course. Although I could have paid more money to extend the time I could take to complete my dissertation, I was bent on avoiding extra cost. A placement in the Oxfam office in Cardiff gave me a feel for the kind of work mostly called for by UK-based development organizations. I wasn't excited by the idea of raising funds and building up donor databases, and my commitment to Richard and his discipleship journey, coupled with the prospect of increasing our family, made the idea of heading overseas to engage in more practical work impossible. We briefly considered a move to London, where there would have been more opportunity to engage in project-based or strategic work. However, we both possessed an innate distaste at the idea of living in the capital, though that was no doubt based on little more than our prejudices.

Perhaps the most logical aspect of our decision not to head to London was that costs seemed insurmountable. Needless to say, if the idea had excited and engaged us, we would have thrown every resource we possessed into making such a move. We felt no such impetus, however, and, believing that the next step needed to be one that caught our enthusiasm and energy, turned our thoughts in a different direction.

That direction also, naturally, needed to include a great deal of consideration of how Richard's calling might now be developed. We therefore returned, perhaps inevitably, to the discussion that had come up briefly before we were married. He still felt there might be a possibility of God calling him to a full-time church ministry, and by this point, the sense of calling was beginning to grow stronger than his fear that it was his own desire, not God's, that was drawing him. We talked about the possibility of him studying at degree level: he had a diploma from the Bible College, but wasn't convinced of his aptitude for tertiary education. However, drawing on my own experience of university study and what I knew of his abilities, I was sure he would be fine. I gave him a gentle push, certain that he was capable, and equally sure that it would help him discover whether this calling might be genuine or not.

So our second year in Swansea was a discussion about the next part of the journey into discovering our calling; a time when I was able to take a part-time job and consider which spiritual shore we might have washed up on following the storms of Belfast; and also a time for us to return to thinking about starting a family. We were not in a position to be financially stable for a good long while, but we weren't considering the matter in a particularly conventional way.

We came to no great conclusions on the spiritual front, other than that we felt that we had finally managed to cast off the guilt we had experienced at our temerity to question the Church's authority and authenticity, and that our anger and desolation had subsided. However, we did make a decision on another front. We decided it was time to start a family. After all, we were young and healthy and saw no point in waiting for a more steady income, since we could not foresee a time when that could possibly happen. Together we also decided that it was time for Richard to study for his degree in theology and began to research courses, locations and all the other myriad details that accompany making such a major change.

That was quite a busy year, looking back on it from this distant perspective. Our first child, Katie, was born in the May, after a long and awkward labour that ended in emergency Caesarean. I graduated from the University of Wales with a Master's in Social Development; and Richard applied through UCAS to study theology at four different universities. To his surprise he was accepted conditionally at three of them, and following an interview at one, he was offered the option to complete the degree within two years instead of three, on the back of his theological studies in Belfast. So other than the bewildering maelstrom of being first-time parents, that year was also about moving to another place that was entirely new to us, in the hope that we were continuing to move toward the centre of where God wanted us to be.

◆   ◆   ◆

Dancing in the rain

And what is faith, but life
in all its pleasures and its pain.
To breathe, to hope, to cry, to love,
to dance in fields of rain.
Where shall I go to find within
the life that faith sets free,
and learn to love the beauty
that my Lover placed in me?
I heard some words of freedom,
then I heard the words again.

And every week I came to seek,
yet I heard the words in vain.
They came to mean no more to me
than colours fading into grey;
they stole each breath that yearned for hope,
and swelled the ocean day by day.
And then I drowned, immersed in words
from which no life or beauty shone.
I felt the choke around my soul:
it seemed as though my light had gone.
But faith is life, and still I love
to dance amidst the falling rain,
and seek the beauty of the One
who gave me breath to breathe again.

In September 2004 we moved to a place called Yeadon, once a village that at some point in the past had been swept into the arms of the Leeds metropolitan borough boundary. We found a three-bedroomed house to rent, and it felt palatial compared to our house in Swansea. Of course, we had no say in the décor, but we furnished it with our small stock of belongings and kind second-hand donations from family. It was originally built to house workers for the mill that had once operated on the tarn across the road, and its age was apparent despite fairly modern fixtures and fittings. Its character was rounded off with a stone stairway leading from the hall down to a cellar below, beneath which flowed an underground stream. Presumably this had been the original water supply to the house, since there was a hole in the floor to access it, but it had in more recent years been equipped with an electric pump to prevent any overflow.

We had fewer practical difficulties with the move to Yeadon than with the previous move. For a start, I found a full-time administrative position at a charity in Bradford that gave us some financial security, and we found a nursery for Katie, close to the college and of excellent reputation. There was every local amenity we could possibly need (a local supermarket and plenty of take-aways—what else is there?), and we settled in well. There were some teething problems with the house: the oven, for instance, had a door that was only precariously balanced on it rather than fixed to it; the gas fire was condemned shortly after we moved in; and the shower, as an electrician informed us not long after we arrived, could have caused us serious injury had it not been fixed. However, we weathered all these things, along with the continuing discovery of the breadth of challenges a tiny baby could present.

I don't think I will ever forget, though, how I felt when Richard and Katie dropped me off at the train station for my first day at work. She was barely three-and-a-half months old: I had spent so much more of my life without her than with her, yet it was such a struggle to see her go. How little I knew then that the sense of constant battle between my roles as carer and provider would only continue to intensify as time went on. The physical side of parenting was tough enough, combining as any parent will know a distinct increase in workload alongside severe sleep disruption. Add in that continual emotional tug-of-war, and therein are encapsulated the greatest challenges of modern parenting.

But I had a fulfilling job, with excellent managers, and Katie was well cared for between Richard and her nursery. We had four good, steady years in Yeadon, marked by a growing confidence in the faith we had begun to rebuild in God—a faith that was less rule-bound, more centred in love and generosity, more inclusive. In general, we had begun to allow God to deal with us more directly, rather than through the intermediaries of church attendance, Bible reading, house group and prayer time. It was here I started the journey towards more consciously understanding God-with-me and recognizing the practice of prayer I was already engaged in. This was conversational prayer, which had become my mainstay, and it was as much a process of becoming more consciously aware that I was doing it as it was about being more deliberate about it. I would simply chat to God at points when my mind was free, perhaps when I was walking or cleaning the house. Subjects would range from anything from the trivial to the deeply theological, and I began to be more purposeful about making space in the dialogue to get some sense of what God might have to say to me.

Richard and I were slowly realizing, however, that the intermediaries were still important, in the context of a new understanding of God in our lives. We had simply come to recognize that God is bigger than the Church, bigger than the Bible, bigger than prayer. This, I suppose, took some courage to acknowledge, because it poses so many more questions than it answers, but for some time by this point I had felt that questions rather than certainties were the meat of my faith. So as part of our preparation for moving to Yeadon we had begun to look for churches nearby—specifically those that might share our now fairly liberal theology, where we could find a spiritual home. Such a possibility seemed unlikely, but we discovered an Anglican church in Leeds that we thought might answer our needs. Introverts as we both are to the core, we breathed in courage from God and took ourselves off one Sunday to test the waters.

We hadn't really considered the implications of bringing a baby to church, and the impact that would have on our ability to concentrate and to join in with the worship. Fortunately, there was another family there with a baby of similar age to our daughter, who helped us to feel a little more at ease than we might have otherwise. We enjoyed the more experimental forms of worship the church offered, which aimed to help the congregation approach God from new angles, creatively and (in theory at least) inclusively. It was a church of the outsider, the dispossessed—several of the congregation had been bruised or felt rejected by the mainstream Church.

Despite our relief at finding a faith community that we could identify with theologically and in worship, we still struggled to feel that we fitted in, even after a year of attending. Perhaps this was because few people in the congregation were equipped to offer teaching and guidance to people experiencing our own particular theological and spiritual vulnerabilities. From my perspective, I felt like a fledgling in the nest, exposed and hungry, sure of what I no longer felt to be true but eager to have more substantial food to replace that which had become bitter in my mouth.

Perhaps it was simply that we never found a "place" within the congregation, but after that first year, we both agreed that it didn't feel as though we had found a spiritual home. We were naturally disappointed and also puzzled: if we weren't able to fit in with people who actually shared our theological outlook, would it be possible for us to fit in anywhere at all?

After making the final decision to stop attending the church in Leeds, we still felt drawn to try re-entering church life and continued to discuss options for doing so. Eventually, in the absence of any good ideas, definite conclusions or hints from God, we decided to return to the traditional model of church attendance and give our local Church of England parish a go. As a denomination it certainly felt like the best possible place for us to find a spiritual home. I was particularly drawn to its encompassing nature, knowing that across the UK, at least, it attracted a wide spectrum of churchmanship. For me, unity was becoming a higher priority than anything relating to what we sang, which instruments accompanied us, whether the prayers were written or ad-libbed, or how long the sermon was. I felt that if the Church of England could embrace Christians on a spectrum from conservative evangelical to high church, therein lay at least a partial reflection of God's nature.

The biggest question that confronted me over the next three years was how it was possible that a church whose theology and worship style most closely matched my own inclinations left me feeling cold, while at my local evangelical congregation I was able to experience the inclusive warmth of a loving, family atmosphere. Attending our local church in Yeadon taught me a great lesson about how much more important people are than ideas. A set of propositions is only as good as the actions it leads you to, in the end. That was a humbling lesson, as was being a part of a congregation that was so generously committed to the community it existed to serve. I was glad that God had brought us there, and glad that I was able to learn those lessons in a place where I felt safe and comfortable—still different, oh, always feeling slightly outside of other people's experience of relationship with God—but learning to accept that feeling because I felt accepted by others for who I was. Looking back now, I suppose I see those three years as my Rivendell.[1] Nowhere since has felt so safe as my church was then. Our second daughter, Bethan, was born while we were there, and we felt that both our children were as fully accepted into the congregation as we were.

But of course, like Frodo resting on his journey to destroy the Ring, we couldn't stay for ever. Despite the challenges and anxieties of life since then, there are many reasons why I am glad we took the next step on our journey.

Once Richard finished his theological degree, with a better result than he ever expected (though I wasn't surprised), we returned to the discussion of his call to full-time ministry. By this stage we were certain of our affiliation to the Church of England and knew that this was the direction we would take if we decided to test this particular path. Having experienced worship and fellowship in a wide range of denominations between us, we felt that the Anglican expression of faith was home for us.

We knew the only way forward was to test the possibility of ordination for Richard, and so he spoke to our vicar and submitted himself for the selection process, taking up a temporary job until the Church of England came to its decision. It was a pretty long process, and it felt even longer because of our eagerness to know what the answer would be. It also suddenly seemed to take up a lot more of Richard's time, which took some adjusting to. I was in a vulnerable state at that stage, as Bethan was born shortly after he began selection, and another event occurred around that time involving a close friend which caused me a great deal of pain and sorrow.

At the time I felt it was over-dramatic to name my emotional state as post-natal depression. Looking back now, I'm more inclined than I was then to think that I at least sailed pretty close to it. I well remember the bereft feeling I was left with until I adjusted to the increased hours Richard had to be away. In theory I knew that God would bring us through all these things to something even better, and it did help me to hold on to hope.

Fast-forward to the spring of 2008, and two events happened within a week of each other in such an incongruous manner that it became difficult to know how to feel. The first was a phone call from my mother, one that I had been expecting for a few months but was not in any way prepared for when it came—my Nanna had died after suffering from dementia for several years. The second was also a phone call, from the Bishop of Bradford to Richard, to let him know that he had successfully completed the selection process and was accepted into ordination training. One so devastating, the other so exciting: both left us with much to think through and plan.

◆   ◆   ◆

A quick recap, then. Between 1999 and 2008 Richard and I had lived in Belfast, Swansea and Yeadon. During this time we had had two daughters (and by now were considering bringing a third child into the mix). We were facing the prospect of moving for his training, then in less than two years returning to Bradford Diocese for a three- to four-year curacy, after which we would move again for his first post. We were still mad enough at that stage to shut our eyes tight and jump in.

The decision over which college to attend for training was a relatively straightforward one. There was a possibility that we could have stayed where we were while Richard travelled daily or weekly to his course, but we never saw that as an option. We felt very much that this calling, though his primarily, was for us as a whole family, because it would require all of us to participate in one way or another. We both wanted to stay in the north, and quite quickly settled on Cranmer College in Durham.

There often isn't much time between being accepted for ordination training and preparing to move. By August that year we were saying goodbye to our home and friends in Yeadon, experiencing again by now almost-familiar sensation of loss coupled with the excitement of the next adventure. We were also, around that time, starting to announce that I was pregnant with child number three, presaging just how wild the next adventure was going to be.

To this day my memory of being in Durham is mostly a blur, with the occasional detail crystallizing out of the fog. For Richard, training consisted of long days and, it must be said, a sense of pressure to take on the chin the enormous amounts of work that he was required to complete. With a degree already under his belt he was put into the Master's programme, alongside which he was required to complete placements and actively participate in college worship. I, meanwhile, had a four-year-old to get settled into school and a twenty-month-old to occupy me at home, as well as undertaking all the usual preparations for welcoming another whole new person into the family.

I had the great benefit of living in a small cul-de-sac with other ordinand families, and enjoying the support of Access, the group for ordinands' spouses. I didn't find a church while we were there, so this group amounted to my spiritual family, and I remain grateful to them to this day. From our next-door neighbours, who also had young children and could sympathize with the stresses particular to an ordinand family; to the older lady who babysat for me so often it felt that she spent more time in my house than hers; to the regular meetings that helped to keep alive in me the knowledge of how important it was to find God in community as well as in solitude;

to the friendships that grew out of belonging to the group; it was valuable to me in these and so many other ways.

During our time in Durham I mostly felt as though I received more care than I gave. That may or may not have been true, but we did experience a certain vulnerability, as Richard dealt with the demands of college life and we prepared ourselves for the new baby arriving.

My experiences of being in labour and giving birth have been by far the most vulnerable times I have known in my life. With little control over my own body and emotions, and with the uncertainties that come with labour, this one was no exception. Katie had eventually been born by emergency Caesarean; I managed to deliver Bethan with assistance after a long labour; what would happen with my third? I desperately wanted to have a completely normal birth, with no intervention, as I was determined that this would be my last. However, although I felt strongly inclined to, I couldn't ask God for such a gift. Never had I wanted something so much that was for me personally and failed to ask for it before then. My inclination was starting to lean quite strongly away from "asking God for stuff" by this time, however, particularly when it came to making personal requests. I had begun to see prayer as something different, and the idea of asking for such a thing felt remarkably indulgent, even making a mockery of my relationship with God, as I was beginning to understand it by then.

I was also beginning to question more widely the purpose and point of intercessory prayer (by which I mean making requests of God on behalf of other people). Not that I would advocate all Christians immediately cease all practice of asking God for blessings for themselves or others; but for me it felt difficult to ask God for anything for anyone at that point in my faith journey, and I think there were several reasons for that.

Firstly, I had become so much more aware of the extent of unmet need right across the globe that it felt unjust to ask for one small blessing in one tiny place that was already so comparatively blessed.

The awakening I had undergone during my Master's course as to the breadth and depth of global and social inequality had only continued to increase in the years following, as I kept abreast of the work of organizations such as Christian Aid and Oxfam. I found it difficult to reconcile the God of such a world with a God who found people parking places when they were desperate.

Secondly, I had become quite reliant on the more conversational kind of prayer I had been developing since my time in Swansea, and felt that this was the only way I was able to offer my genuine presence to God. I found that intercession and petition left me feeling suffocated, distanced, removing all sense of life from my otherwise thriving relationship with him.

Thirdly (and looking back, probably resulting at least in part from the first and second causes), it felt as though the foundation of my relationship with God had shifted quite radically since my time in Belfast. My young faith had been very dependent on the teaching I had received from the Church, and that rug had largely been pulled out from under my feet; since moving to Swansea I had been consciously and subconsciously having to work out on my own what was more important and what was less so in my faith. Prayer was a big part of that, and in some ways I was probably still rebelling against the Church's insistence that "every Christian should study their Bible and pray every day". It was as though I was a teenager breaking away from my parents' authority and learning about the world on my own terms. Praying in the way that I felt to be most life-giving was an urgent necessity to me, and the remains of what the Church had once offered as valid spirituality were nothing more than a dried husk.

Having my third child, then, was quite a crucial stage in my developing relationship with God. It taught me about how I saw God, and prayer, and myself in God, and I suppose I'm only now beginning to realize how valuable that was. It transpired that I was able to deliver my son, Daniel, naturally, without any intervention: make what you will of that.

A related struggle I was engaging with at the time was the concept of God's "plan", which I felt was commonly seen as a path of events that he supposedly has mapped out for each of his followers. I had tussled with this question on and off during my entire Christian life and it had now returned to confront me again. Decisions about relationships, housing, careers, family, holidays—you name it, I grew into my faith with the expectation leaning on me that in such matters, God's decision was final, and it was our duty to decode his wishes for us and make sure we put them into practice. I have seen perfectly intelligent people brought to a confused standstill because they are too honest to say that they can't work out what God wants; others wrap themselves up in self-delusion, because they are unable to be that honest. I have fallen into both categories myself, and having begun to recognize such weakness in myself, I found my time in Durham was a ripe opportunity for attempting a more nuanced approach to discerning what God wanted for me.

I now had three children. It was crystal clear to Richard and me that three was enough, thank you very much. I knew I had a few years to go before I would be in any position to return to work, but that didn't stop my mind from engaging with the question—what was my purpose and calling, the one I thought I had discerned all those years ago in Belfast but that had seemed to slip like sand through my fingers? Of all the different things I had done—from an outsider's perspective, a random series of work and study choices—out of all that rich soil, what would rise up? I was impatient to know, yet reluctant to be told where to go and what to do like an errant child. It felt as though my relationship with God had progressed beyond that stage, into something more mature—perhaps into a place in which I felt able to recognize that he trusted me with the abilities he had given me. I felt treasured, and loved, and protected by him, and perhaps it was this that gave me the courage I needed to break free of the reliance on "being told what to do" that we all crave because in a hard world, it is so much easier than having to work it out for ourselves.

I didn't have any complete answers by the end of my time in Durham, but I did have one potential piece of the puzzle. Through the spouses' group I was introduced to St Antony's Priory, an ecumenical retreat house and spirituality centre not far from where we lived. The Priory offered spiritual direction to individuals who sought it, and I came upon this little-known ministry around the time that I realized my prayer life needed new direction and input. The further one moves away from church-based prayer and worship, the harder it is to find resources to inform one's prayer life; so despite the logistical difficulties of childcare I committed to seeing a spiritual director once a month for the last nine months of our time in Durham.

Chapter 3

Origami

Imagine a piece of paper
bigger than the sky,
folded into a puzzle
that fits in the palm of your hand.
Imagine the eternity it would take
to lift each fold,
smooth out the creases,
and uncover the complexity
of patterns and pictures
with which it is adorned.
Imagine the tender,
creative Love
that with gentle hands and delicate movements
undertakes the task of unfolding.
I don't need to imagine
the tools with which Love works,
for they are here, with me.

I remain convinced to this day that spiritual direction (also known as spiritual accompaniment or having a soul friend[2]) is a ministry that every Christian should have the opportunity to experience. There is something immensely precious about being given an hour away from all distractions, in which your spiritual director gently accompanies you on the journey towards an ever-deepening relationship with God. The best directors are excellent listeners, not just hearing but absorbing; they listen to God themselves to know when to be silent and when to speak; they know how to suggest, when to be gentle and when to be strong, because they commit to setting their own selves aside for that hour to focus fully on facilitating your conversation with God.

I was very fortunate: my spiritual director, although she had had only recently finished her training, had a great depth of empathy and insight. She taught me some new ways to pray that opened up so many more possibilities to me, such as praying with my imagination, or with the Bible, or simply through increasing my awareness of being in the world around me that God had created. I began to recognize more consciously that I liked—and preferred—solitude, and to create opportunities where possible to enjoy time alone to pray. In a home with an extremely busy husband and three children under the age of six, such opportunities were a profound blessing when they came. My prayer life remained largely informal and unstructured, but it began to lead me out of the shallows and into a deeper part of the pool.

Perhaps the most profound consequence of beginning to receive spiritual direction was the awakening of an idea that it might be something I could offer to others. Very near the end of my nine months with my spiritual director I tentatively raised the subject, and received enough encouragement to begin seriously considering the possibilities. I knew that a course was being offered at St Antony's Priory beginning in the January after we were to leave. Feeling so attuned to the physical space and to the atmosphere of the place I was keen to train there if I could, despite the potential logistical difficulties. It was to take place over six months, and involved day-long workshops twice a month, and two weekends away, which would have implications for Richard's work as well. Therefore a lot of thought had to go into whether and how such a thing could be done. Since we were also confronted with another house move and city move, I left making that particular decision until we were settled in our next parish.

◆   ◆   ◆

When an ordinand's course is only two years long, they must start to consider where they will serve their curacy less than twelve months after they begin training. We were considering where we might move to next before Daniel was even born; we felt we would like to move back to Bradford Diocese, and so began our enquiries there, wondering how long it would take until we knew where we were going and could begin to make plans for our next move. At this stage, the reality of two more house moves within the next four to five years (a curacy is usually only three to four years long) was beginning to press on us; we were very eager to make each transition with as little fuss and worry as possible.

We were very pleasantly surprised that Richard was one of the first ordinands to find out where they were going; we hadn't stipulated much beyond the fact that we didn't want to live in a city centre, but since during the process we were asked to imagine what our ideal parish would look like, we had said that a large village or market town would suit us quite well. When he was placed in Ilkley, we were delighted. It was only half an hour from our old church, so we would have friends not far away. It was a beautiful location, with a choice of schools, and a perfectly sufficient town centre which would meet most of our needs. And so, once the last essay was written and the final exam sat; once Richard had found out that he had passed everything and was allowed to be ordained deacon; once the house was purchased and prepared for us, then off we headed for a new adventure, and a new phase in our life together.

There were some difficulties for us to manage on our arrival in Ilkley. Compared to the experiences of many of Richard's cohort they were reasonably solvable, however. For us, it helped that our training incumbent and the congregation were welcoming and supportive. Our biggest difficulty was getting our eldest daughter a school place within Ilkley (we had failed to consider the fact that we were moving somewhere people often move to in order to get their children into a particular school!). Instead, we were offered a school place at a village three miles away. It seemed ridiculous that we lived and worked in Ilkley but could not school our child there, so we appealed, and were eventually successful. However, the administration of the appeal was handled so clumsily that Katie had to miss two weeks of school after we arrived until the decision was made. It is hard to appreciate the effect of such an event until one experiences it first-hand, but the uncertainty and stress, and particularly the delay in being able to settle into those essential routines that help to bring calm to daily life, had a longer-term effect than I liked on the process of becoming part of our new home town.

For a number of reasons, perhaps the most influential being my own disinclination, I had not attended a church regularly in Durham. To take two, then three small children on my own (as Richard always had placements on a Sunday) into a situation that would require a vat-full of energy to acclimatize the children to, when I was still suffering an unshakeable antipathy towards church attendance, turned out to be too much to ask. So I didn't. And as far as I can remember, I didn't feel particularly bad about it either. I had enjoyed rewarding fellowship with the spouses' group I had belonged to, and the children had all become a part of that "church family".

But that decision had consequences that I hadn't foreseen. Suddenly, Richard was a curate at a large family church, and I knew that it was important for us as a family that we become a part of the congregation. I had a six-year-old, a three-year-old and a one-year-old, and I hadn't had a great deal of experience with shepherding children through a Sunday service. Despite the progress I had made towards forgiving the Church during our time in Yeadon, I still struggled with an antipathy towards church services, perhaps largely because I never felt able to meet God in them. And so I found my first few months were dominated by managing the tension between that antipathy and my desire to support Richard.

I don't think attending church services with children, especially toddlers and babies, is ever easy. On reflection, it is no wonder that my natural disinclination for church services intensified over that time. God and Church had become so far separated in my mind that I could enjoy my faith, my lived relationship with God, even while struggling to come to terms with what was required of me as a curate's wife and a mother. It took a good six months to get used to the rhythm of getting out of the house on a Sunday morning and to get the children used to the idea of attending Sunday School.

I also revisited the question of taking on the spiritual direction course in Durham once we had moved. Since the idea had strong support from both Richard and the incumbent vicar, who was aware of the impact it would have on Richard's schedule, I decided to go ahead. I felt some trepidation, having been warned of the rigorous nature of the course and how much self-examination would be required. Mostly, though, I was full of excitement, eager for every session, and facing up to each challenge with complete confidence in God's ability to guide me through it. There were some important things to learn about myself, but it seemed that I responded very positively to that unfolding process, and it drew my relationship with God into an even more intimate and loving phase. The course was also of immense value in helping me understand the depth of my calling to the ministry of spiritual direction, and I have been offering it to others ever since.

After completing the course, Daniel became old enough for pre-school, which meant two and a half hours of freedom for me every weekday morning. I was never the sort of mother who pines after her children—rather, I revelled in the space to breathe, and find out who I was again. This had the effect of making me feel a little guilty to begin with, but when I realized that I felt I had to apologize for not missing my children, I had to have stern words with myself. The last thing I needed was to lock myself in a cage of cultural parenting expectations.

I don't think I'm alone in experiencing quite a radical loss of self after becoming a mother. Having spoken to other women about the subject, I'm sure that each of us loses at least a part of ourselves in the face of the total need and vulnerability of a new-born baby. It took me quite some time to recognize the extent to which I had submerged myself, but in the space away from Daniel I began to get a glimpse. I noticed it had become more difficult to identify my own inclinations and desires, and the simple question, "What do you want to do?" had become remarkably difficult to answer.

I hadn't made an attempt to re-enter the workplace at this stage, partly because I knew we would be moving again before long and partly because we were comfortable enough on the income we had. I used that free time instead to take walks in the woods and by the river, and to develop my writing. I began to write more poetry again, a pastime that had become a casualty of motherhood. One fanzine I subscribed to asked to print one of them, which put me in touch with an established poet, who encouraged me to write more. I even began entering poems into competitions and submitting them to magazines.

Work, and particularly earning power, were starting to become pressing questions for me as well though. I began to realize that, given Richard's diary and the needs of the children, an office-based job was impractical, particularly since I was unlikely to be able to command a salary that would make it worthwhile. I wanted to be at home for the children as much as possible; I wanted to be able to work within school hours and school terms, and have control over the amount of work that I did. These were all ideas in their infancy at this point in time, since I had decided to wait until Daniel was in school before actively exploring work options. But at least the ideas gave direction to my thoughts, and pointed me towards considering which of my skills and experiences could be applied to some kind of self-employment.

◆   ◆   ◆

Chance meeting

In the first blush of spring
I met you; a carven statue of bare branch and bough,
clothing your nudity in borrowed foliage.
You rose out of the undergrowth, shy,
yet unable to hide the smooth, straight beauty
of your trunk, your crooked arms
raised to the sky.
Through shadow and into glorious light
you stretched yourself, aching for the divine,
delighting in the rich gifts of sun and soil.
I passed by and you reached to
brush my shoulder,
twigs pulsing with the promise of spring-life,
buds bursting to unfold and embrace
all heaven's gifts.
You said, "Here I am, in this with you. Together we
hold the Earth and the sky;
the soil feeds us and the air breathes us.
We are gift to each other, bestowed by another,
blessing this moment in time."

At the same time as exploring these questions of identity and work, I found myself enjoying possibly the richest period I had ever experienced in my relationship with God, perhaps largely as a result of the spiritual direction course. Having reached a point at which I had finally become comfortable to some degree with the concept of my own freedom to be and to become in Christ; where I had learned to revel in God's generosity; where I had become so attuned to the pulse of the Earth that it felt as though God was breathing life into me through its rhythm. I found that prayer had become as natural as being, and my trust in God and his presence with me was as complete as I ever anticipated it was possible to be.

Of particular significance was my discovery of the concept of contemplative, or silent, prayer. I had been introduced to several forms of imaginative prayer during my course, but contemplation is the prayer that requires us to set aside all thoughts and images, to (eventually) enter the silent space in which God meets us in the most profound way possible. This was the prayer of the fourteenth-century mystics and, indeed, goes even further back in Christian history, almost to the earliest followers of Christ. I attempted it myself, though with insufficient discipline to do so regularly, but even in those early stages I recognized a particular affinity with that form of prayer.

◆   ◆   ◆

All the while I was making these explorations for myself, Richard was acclimatizing to the rhythm of church life and the demands of a large and active congregation. As a curate he was responsible to his training incumbent, and the parish also benefited from a good number of readers and retired clergy. I didn't realize how valuable this was until we moved away! We eventually settled into a reasonably workable routine, and as far as is ever possible, became more used to the longer hours and higher levels of energy required by his work. However, at the beginning of 2012 a series of difficulties began to present themselves that tested us beyond any limits we ever could have imagined that we had.

Very early in the year, Richard found out that there was some worry about his father's health, in that he might have Alzheimer's disease. With his family all in Northern Ireland, this was a very difficult truth to come to terms with, and it was the first event of the year that confronted us with the challenge of understanding something to be real that you are unable to see with your own eyes.

Hot on the heels of that announcement, we were informed that Richard's training incumbent had accepted a post elsewhere and would be leaving after that Easter. This was initially quite a shock:

he had been at the church only three years, and it was quite an unexpected move. Even once we had had time to get used to the idea, we both remained anxious about the increased workload Richard would have to undertake until a new vicar was appointed. But, with little choice in the matter, we both took a long, deep breath and, following the Easter break, plunged into the new reality as positively as we could.

Then, not two months later, came the worst news we had ever received. Richard's mother, Margaret, was ill with pancreatic cancer; she was at stage four, and had between three and six months to live.

I still remember vividly the day Richard told me. The children were raising a cacophony in the kitchen-diner of our small townhouse, all three making demands that instantly needed to be met, and I had to ask him to pause so that I could settle them enough to be able to hear. He said the words, and they somehow meant nothing to me. There was simply a wall that appeared somehow between my lived experience and comprehension of the forthcoming death of my mother-in-law.

At this point I lose the capacity to find words that will adequately describe the experience of the following weeks and months. We had to plan a visit at the earliest opportunity, to take the children over to see their Granny, probably for the very last time. Daniel, the youngest, was only three years old, but still it felt important to try and secure him some kind of memory of her. At that point we thought it could well be the last chance they would have to see her alive, and we were almost right.

Somehow we had to keep going; make all the small, everyday decisions that now seemed to weigh disproportionately heavily on us. I worried deeply about Richard, bearing responsibility that he had not been prepared for in work, and having to struggle through this agonizing period of waiting at the same time. The one mote of light during that grey-fog time was the care and concern of our church community. After we had survived a week in Northern Ireland in July, they raised a generous amount of money that allowed Richard to return on his own several times in the last few weeks of his mother's life.

Then came the call we had been dreading. Margaret didn't have much time left. We decided in the end to all go over together by car and ferry—it was a tough decision, since we weren't sure whether we would get there in time. But it turned out to be the best decision in the end.

The hardest part for me at that point, strangely, was going to the children's school and informing the office that we were taking them over to Northern Ireland and why. The receptionist was so matter-of-fact about the news. I had found it incredibly painful to speak the words out loud to her, and quite why she seemed to take it so blankly I struggled to comprehend. It seemed as though the pain I felt should have been screaming through the ground and all the people around me. Somehow, life simply carried on.

So that third week in September we all piled into our big behemoth of a car for the long drive to Stranraer. I drove for the first leg—but we'd only been going half an hour when I felt as though there was something not quite right about the accelerator. Somehow it just didn't respond in the way it ought to, and so I pulled over.

Once I'd stopped the car, there was no starting it again. We had to call for roadside assistance—already nervous about arriving at the ferry terminal on time, struggling through numbness and exhaustion, we somehow had to wait patiently and encourage the children to remain patient too. It took maybe an hour for the recovery vehicle to arrive; the driver towed us to a place where he could examine the car more easily, took a good look, and then told us that his advice would be to turn around and take the car to a garage for repairs. There was a leak in the cooling system, and it would cause damage to the engine if we tried to continue driving.

So, we then had to tell him the purpose of our journey. Why is it that telling strangers such news is somehow worse than telling those you know? It's as though the telling reacquaints you with the truth again, freshly painted with the pain you had hoped you would at least start to become acclimatized to.

The mechanic was very sympathetic, and honest with us. He was obliged to inform us of his formal advice, and we had to sign a piece of paper to say that we had decided against taking it; but he also told us that we could manage to keep going if we stopped often enough to fill up the water tank; that the car would at least get us to where we needed to go, as long as we were careful. The gratitude I continue to feel to this day for his kind honesty is unmeasurable—even beginning to contemplate alternative travel arrangements felt devastating, as it seemed that the only option would be to split up, so that Richard could get over quickly, and we would follow on as best we could. This way we were able to continue on together, anxious about the car, but at least able to support one another.

Given the delay in our journey we knew we had missed our ferry, but fortunately were able to change the booking to sail on the next one. The day felt as thin and stretched as an old pair of tights, and by the time we arrived in Belfast, around 11 o'clock that night, we had gone beyond exhaustion into some kind of bleary haze. But Margaret was still alive. Richard went straight to the hospice to see her, and I was left to settle the children to sleep and stare into the vacant abyss of grief until the mercy of sleep overtook me.

The next morning the children and I went to the hospice to visit Margaret. Richard and I felt it was important for them to see her still alive, to help them remember her as she had been and to help them grieve once she died. She was by this time largely unconscious, highly dosed on morphine, and so not able to respond to us, but we knew that we could talk to her and on some level she would understand us. Family members said they had seen physical responses from her when they had talked to her. So we took the children in, one by one, and talked as though it was a normal family visit, telling her what each of them had been up to, getting them to talk out loud if they felt able to. Then it was my turn.

I wanted to be strong, and cheerful, and help to make her remaining hours as bearable as possible. I read her a couple of my poems, and told her about my writing and how it was getting on. To this day I fiercely wish I hadn't started crying, but I needed to tell her how much I loved her, that we would miss her so raggedly for "a little while" until we all met up again—and through those words the tears came. I saw her leg jerk; I knew she had recognized my grief and didn't want to upset her further. The care assistant came in, so I left her, aware that this was probably the last goodbye.

What did we do next? I have no memory. Probably spent time with the family, who were gathering in groups in each other's houses, waiting, waiting . . . now quiet and then full of words, now laughing at old memories, then lapsing into silence and sorrow. We must have existed somehow for the next day and a half, and still she hung on, until the Sunday evening, just after 7 o'clock. She was surrounded by family when she died—I was at our niece's house looking after the children, but my elder sister- and brother-in-law, after spending some time at the hospice, returned fairly late and offered me the car to go and be with Richard, and his mother's body.

I had never seen a dead body before. I was anxious about that, but somehow, knowing that the family were all there, with grief more direct and fierce and raw than mine, but finding strength in each other's company, made it a little easier. I walked into her room, and there they all were: husband, children, sisters, sons- and daughters-in-law, an aura of calm sorrow about them—she had had a difficult and painful end, had perhaps struggled to let go of life, and perhaps unconsciously even then they felt her relief at relinquishing her suffering. They were all sat in a circle—how vividly I remember!—I hadn't seen my younger sister-in-law at that point, and we hugged, and she sobbed. Then I had to look at Margaret's body, to touch her cold hand, and realize with finality that she had gone.

◆   ◆   ◆

Black suit

I have to buy a black suit;
I have to write an epitaph
of grief, and love, and hope untold
to publish in the Telegraph.
I have to see the sorrow deep
within my husband's eyes, and watch
resolve take hold, while love unfolds
in broken, bitter-sweet goodbyes.
And though no ties of blood demand
my loyalty to his mother's life,
love grows in time; it roots and twines
itself between such disparate hearts.
And as she slowly fades towards
the dark, uncertain path ahead,
I fear the howl of pain that gathers
in the tears I've left unshed.
I have to buy a black suit;
I have to write an epitaph.
I have to hope that love endures
beyond the grief and earth and ash.

The funeral was arranged in less than a week, and still I can't remember what we did in the intervening time. I don't suppose there's any way the dreary details would find prominence in my thoughts—those events that stand out are the ones in which time or emotion are distilled, concentrated by the intensity of feeling within them. So, for instance, the funeral, which felt to me was designed less to support a family in their grief and more to proselytize those mourners who, by some slim chance, might not have heard the gospel before.

I was angry then, and even now I am still left with the unsettled feeling that something at the funeral wasn't quite completed. I can't help thinking that it has at least in part been the reason why Richard and I have found it so difficult to grieve. However, the service was held at the mission hall that Margaret had regularly attended, which was packed with so many people whose lives she had touched—I was overwhelmed by the number of people there. Close family attended the burial (cremations are still relatively rare in Northern Ireland); the coffin was winched into the ground, the dust thrown, the words spoken, and we returned to the hall, where members of the mission hall had provided a generous supper. And so, in some strange dichotomy, it felt as though there was loving welcome as well as spiritual rebuff, which I can now reflect is probably a fairly common experience for those who encounter or engage with the Church.

◆   ◆   ◆

We spent nine days in Northern Ireland in total. We returned to Ilkley, and at that point, if not sooner, my powers of empathy appeared to shut down. I could no longer rely on my intuition to help me understand and engage with people, not even (especially not) my husband and children. I felt no more than a slight twinge when, after attempting to take some time off, Richard returned to work after only two weeks. Had I not been deep in the maelstrom of grief, that decision would have concerned me much more deeply.

But I couldn't see much at all. It felt as though a weight was attached to my forehead that dragged my head downward so that the ground beneath my feet was the only thing within my field of vision. I operated on automatic, every action costing an enormous amount of energy and will to perform—I remember well the exhaustion with which I faced planning Bethan's birthday celebrations that October. Christmas was little better. I dragged myself away for a few days' retreat the following January, and it provided me with some much-needed space to give attention to my grief; and yet I didn't consider myself to be grieving badly. I was simply numb, consumed by an all-encompassing grey fog, and waiting for the time when I would be able to see and feel again.

I knew, beyond doubt, that God was in the numbness with me. So full of life had I been before this grief that my confidence in him was complete; when the numbness lifted, as I was sure it would in due course, that relationship would re-establish itself. I was clear in my mind that how I felt in those months was a natural part of grieving, and though the sensation of God's presence was missing, it would just as naturally return once I was able to see again.

Part 2: Absence

Chapter 4

Grief's grace-offering

The other day I woke
as if from a dream of ineffable sadness;
tendrils of disbelieving loss remained,
the dream-tears dry on my cheek
and a void where pain should be.
And then, with more effort than I understood,
I lifted my eyes above the earth and gravestone
to where you stood, immersed in filial grief.
In that still moment,
my eyes adjusting to a new lens,
I recognized release—and once again I could see
not only you but also me.
And there it flashed across my sight—
a veiled tang and glint of sharpened edge;
I saw grief's wicked parting blow,
the stake it drove between our fragile hearts.
Or perhaps the turning in to self
was grief's grace-offering to pain—
a scab upon the wound of severed love
that one day falls away.

I can still remember the almost physical sensation I experienced at
the end of that grey-fog period of grieving, which lasted about six
months all told. One day I realized that the weight that had been
dragging my head down was gone, almost without me noticing, and

it felt as though I was able to look up again. The first thing I saw, properly, was my husband in his own grief.

Having returned to the point at which I could "see" the world around me, and the lives of those in it, my automatic belief was that my previously-experienced relationship with God would reinstate itself and that he would be here with me again, intimately concerned with every aspect of my life. As ever, he would be at my side to share my still-progressing grief and help me with what felt like the enormous responsibility of helping Richard and the children work through their own. And beyond the serious, even to be there for the everyday to-and-fro of thought and reflection and easy conversation that had been a natural part of our relationship for so long.

It took perhaps a couple of months for me to realize that my expectations of what would happen were not playing out. Looking back from this vantage point, how could things have "reverted to normal" after such a near and sharp and life-altering loss? Of course, there was no way I could have guessed how things would develop; my assumptions were based on what I knew about how God responds to those in pain and suffering, and I thought I'd acquired a pretty thorough knowledge of the fullness of his love for his children.

Now, looking back, I can't remember the moment when I realized that it felt as though he had completely withdrawn from me. I suspect I buried the memory of it somewhere, because it was too painful to carry consciously along with my grief and worry and concern for my family.

The essence of this experience continued with me in one form or another for several years. How I responded to the feeling of abandonment shifted and altered throughout those years, sometimes for good and sometimes for bad, but the simple fact was that God—who was a very real, authentic figure to me, and a vitally important part of my life—appeared to have walked off, or to have been carried away by the grey fog when it lifted and allowed me to see out of my grief again.

The rest of this book will examine what it has been like to live a life of faith without the sense that my faith and love were being reciprocated. This is not a complete, how-to-survive-God's-absence primer, in which everything is finished, the last "t" crossed, the last "i" dotted. This is not a book of answers: it is a book about experience and questions. Never was the ability to hold questions without demanding answers more vital to sustaining my faith than during that dark time, but there were times when I doubted whether I even had that ability any longer. I had no security that I would live to see the day when I would experience God's love again rather than just assent to it intellectually, and at times I despaired that it would ever happen; yet, through it all, I have found that hope has eventually prevailed each time despair has threatened to drown me in darkness.

◆   ◆   ◆

Dark prayer

Long ago,
you bruised me on the altar
of your promise to me.
I bore its rough stone
upon my shoulders, yet you weakened
the pillar-bases—
I watched each one crumble,
now slowly, now
flicking away in an unremembered instant.
The altar-top fell
in pieces, left its wound,
and out of the steep darkness

> of my centre I cried
> for you to keep me.
> You reached out and caught
> the fine thread of that prayer,
> found ways to weave strength
> into its faint plea—
> found ways to uncover
> what you had written of me.
> In time the bruise began to fade,
> and I knew what it was to be yours again.
> How could I have known
> that after bruising comes the breaking?
> I was not brittle, nor delicate.
> You had woven me with strong cord.
> And yet I stand here,
> straining my eyes across a vast, stone landscape,
> watching as you smash me, like a ball of glass,
> and my pieces scatter
> without a thread to hold them in between.
> And I am not what I have been.
> Where is my dark prayer now?
> Is it spinning towards your open hands,
> and will you, once again, hold onto me?

The conscious acceptance that God was somehow not with me, despite being with me, marked a profound change in my spiritual journey. I gradually began to understand that something foundational was shifting in my understanding of God, the world and my place in it. It began with disquiet but relative peace: my initial assumption was that yes, in my numbness God was absent, but the experience was merely a symptom of grief, and as my emotional strength returned, so too would my relationship with God be restored. I gave little thought at the time as to why

I considered grief to be a powerful enough sedative to sever my spirit from God.

It was late spring of the year following Margaret's death that I began to acknowledge this "absence experience" might be something more than simply grief-spun. One or two entries in my journal during that winter and spring include tentative references to feeling not just numb, but bereft of God. The feeling grew insistent enough that, heading towards the summer months, I began examining it in the light of the "dark night" experience as described by St John of the Cross.[3] At the time it felt like a profound presumption, to be placing my spiritual "status" on a par with one of the great mystics. The feeling that I might be indulging in an ego-driven exercise left me quite hesitant to pursue the idea, and I tried to assume that it was my grief and stress that were causing this experience.

I began to realize, however, that although my grief had passed through its first, intense phase and was becoming something more manageable, there was no change in the feeling that God had taken himself away from me. If anything, that feeling only intensified as I continued to regain something approaching equilibrium. Alongside it, to add to the welter of concern and anxiety, was a growing sense of being overwhelmed by the extent of pain and suffering not just in my life but in the world. It is a (bad) habit of mine to go through occasional phases of consuming news as though it is an addiction, and this was one of them. Possessing an ongoing concern for social justice and human rights, I usually keep information channels (both mainstream and social media) open to events happening globally and locally. I ordinarily view this as both a blessing and a curse: at that time, it was merely a curse. I can only describe it as feeling like the weight of it pressed all the air out of my lungs until I was breathless; and the recognition that God had to suffer this all the time, without ceasing, without comfort, was unbearable.

◆   ◆   ◆

It may or may not be of significance that the beginning of this tumultuous spiritual experience also marked the beginning of my attempts to forge a new place for myself in the world of work. I am inexpressibly grateful that because of Richard's vocation I was able to take my time over this, and the demands of making an income didn't have to override my strong desire to explore how my own vocation might unfold. My explorations had in part begun the previous summer, when a poet for whom I had held a long-standing admiration happened to read one of my poems. Remarkably, this was followed by an opportunity to meet said poet, not just once, but twice that year; and not only to meet, but to enter into a correspondence that continues to give me the confidence to pursue my writing today.

Following the establishment of this—mentorship, I suppose you would call it—I was very keen to explore what possible avenues I could through my writing. This led me to develop a more disciplined approach to writing and submitting, and brought me, that summer, to one of the richest and most fulfilling literary experiences of my life. I undertook a week-long course in poetry run by the Arvon Foundation, based at Ted Hughes' old house on the side of a breathtakingly beautiful valley in West Yorkshire. Although it occurred at a time of great emotional and spiritual vulnerability, it nevertheless challenged and encouraged me in my writing, and provided further confirmation to me that this was something that could be a possible career option.

Along with the spiritual and literary challenges of 2013, as a family we were also facing the prospect of another relocation. I felt particularly for my eldest daughter, who had already moved primary schools once, and I was intensely relieved that after the next move we would be able to remain for as long as we pleased. I felt exhausted at the very idea of moving house and location again, but was determined to throw as much energy into it as possible, despite the generally low ebb of my spirits. I was so very eager to arrive at the moment when we would be able to say: we are here, and we do not have to leave.

Richard found a post in a village in East Yorkshire that appealed very much to both of us. It was in many ways idyllic, and we had to remind ourselves that there is no perfect parish quite regularly in order to frame our enthusiasm within a more realistic outlook. He was successful at interview, impressing the panel over and above candidates from within that diocese, and when he was offered the post we were both delighted for him to accept it.

The move, however, in the October of 2013, did nothing to mask the ongoing spiritual nadir I found myself in. With God still stubbornly absent, I began to make reference in my journal to a sense that my "self" was suffering annihilation—that somehow, the substance of me was disappearing. Alongside that, I was writing about the difficulties I found with being honest in my journal entries. It was as though writing down how I felt was self-indulgent, an exercise in giving in to feelings that I was at risk of misinterpreting. I struggled to identify where that sense came from, since to that point I had always found my journal to be the safest place I had in which to fully express everything that is inside me. The spiritual confusion I felt was perhaps a reflection of the confusion that is always flung like handfuls of cotton thread into the air when one uproots and has to re-establish oneself in a new place. Yet there was the odd moment of clarity. Only a couple of weeks before the actual move I found myself lucid enough to ask: *does God still love me?*

◆   ◆   ◆

It was a much easier move than the previous one: there was no trouble with getting the children into their new school, which was less than a stone's throw from our house; the church congregation was smaller, which meant fewer names to learn, and like our previous parish, was warm and welcoming, and incredibly supportive of us finding our own place and purpose, rather than trying to impose expectations on us. Finally, moving to a much larger house and garden pleased all of us a great deal. Perhaps we felt we could breathe a little more deeply.

Questions of faith and relationship with God were no less pressing than they had been for the previous six months, but they continued to be framed within the context of a life that placed high demands on me both physically and emotionally. "Setting up house", creating something manageable out of the wildness of the garden, exploring the ever-existing question of my so-far non-existent career and discovering what it meant for me to be a "vicar's wife" gave me plenty to do. Yet while all this taxed me, still the questions about where God was, why he had apparently abandoned me and what could I do to fix it remained painfully present.

It is difficult to describe how thoroughly the weight of those questions became absorbed into my everyday experience. I went through what seemed to be a never-ending cycle of raging refusal to accept the reality of it, to defeated, partial acceptance that left me in some very dark places indeed, and back to rage, over and over. Anyone who has been through this experience will know that it is utterly, utterly exhausting. It drains your physical, emotional and spiritual energy and leaves you bereft of any sense of value in life. I have at times been astonished at the fact that I still managed to continue my daily tasks, given how little point there seemed to be in any of it.

And yet, life still continued. In 2014, I suppose when I still believed that this absence would simply absent itself one day, I made a few advances in my writing. I found freelance work writing human rights articles for an online magazine, and I also had a poem accepted for publication in a national poetry magazine. Then, having dipped my toe in the water, I quite quickly stepped back again, realizing that the prospect of building up any steady income as a writer would likely take much more time than I felt was available, given that one of my priorities was to contribute to the family income sooner rather than later.

During the same period I was also invited to join an ecumenical team that delivered prayer and spirituality events in Hull and the East Riding. I accepted the invitation despite feeling as though I was sorely underqualified and that it might be a stretch too far of my time and inner resources. What called me to the work was firstly the opportunity it offered me to connect with other like-minded people; secondly, being able to participate in opening up people's horizons in their prayer lives; and thirdly, the chance to develop my skills and experience in the field. It felt particularly important in light of the incredible sense of fulfilment that spiritual direction had offered to me.

During that year, however, further losses contributed to my sense of alienation from God. While there was no communication between God and me, one or two avenues of possible connection through intermediaries had remained open to that point: a person whose honesty about the things of God I had long trusted in; and a place I was used to going in which I had always felt safe in being able to explore the furthest reaches and ragged edges of my faith. In the spring of 2014, a course of events was set in motion that succeeded in destroying both of these cradles of my faith. I was numb with shock in the aftermath of these revelations, and it took many months for me to recognize how thoroughly those faith supports had been stripped from me.

That was also the year that my struggle with those questions of human suffering reached its peak. It came to me in waves that would render me almost breathless, until it felt as though I was experiencing some small inkling of the pain that God must know in bearing that suffering. I wasn't mired in bitterness and resentment then, and felt both a desperate urge to be able to comfort God, and a terrible impotence, since this was one thing I simply couldn't do.

Even the moon is hiding tonight

Even the moon is hiding tonight
behind clouds that are tenderly clothed by her light.
Yet their luminous comfort is no safe retreat
from the drum-roll of death below, pounding its beat.
She continues to turn, and to steward the tide,
but she fearfully longs to find somewhere to hide
from the hollowing ache at the things she has seen;
the suffering silence that falls in between
the one and the other, the pride and the fall,
the gun and the knife-blade, the thirty-foot wall,
the panic, the game-plan, the uncontained rage,
the drone and the sniper, the reinforced cage.
For her memory fills like a limitless pool,
which runs red with the blood shed by every last fool
who thought fear was a safe place, a price to be paid
for the glory of leading the victors' parade.
Now the clouds pass the moon: she can no longer shield
from the bite of the weapon despair likes to wield
in each dread-girdled story; each sewer-dark jail;
each merciful impulse repressed till it's stale.
The nebulous darkness embraces her pain,
and whispers its solace while circling again
to the daybreak that stretches too far from her eyes;
though from Earth, she shines pure in
    the morning-dressed skies.

◆   ◆   ◆

By November of 2014 I had begun to recognize some of the deeper
consequences of an ongoing experience of God's absence, and the
continued dissolution of so much of the foundation that my faith
had been built upon. This recognition began with the realization

that I had lost something I probably hadn't previously realized I possessed, but that now I think we all have: a narrative, a story we tell ourselves to make sense of the world around us and within us. Everything we think and feel and experience is anchored into this narrative, and that anchoring provides security. Sometimes new events cause us to edit or redraft the story to some extent, but certainly in my lifetime, up until then, I had never known that narrative to be absent. And yet there it was, a gaping hole—a darkness in which I had no harness or torch. I wasn't falling, but I didn't feel safe, and I didn't feel as though there was anywhere I could turn to for comfort. That realization left me overwhelmed with loneliness and isolation, and with little hope for any change.

Out of that realization of lost narrative, I recognized two further consequences of God's absence. The first was that I was struggling to make any sense of who God was; the second was that I had, by and large, lost any sense of who I was as well. I think actually recognizing and naming this awareness was quite important though, as with each "discovery" I have made, it led me to hope that I cracked the problem and had found a way forward that would "fix" everything. Not so. Taking a quiet day at a retreat centre in December that year, I tried to come up with even a few things I could say I knew for certain about God, and I experienced an inner resistance to the exercise that startled me in its implacability. It seemed, for the time being at least, that both God and I needed to remain deconstructed, until such time as I was ready to begin the project of rebuilding. One thing, however, that became clearer to me than ever as a result of that quiet day, was that knowledge of self and knowledge of God are inextricably linked, and that the journey of discovering those two identities is at the very core of relationship with God.

By the spring of 2015, I became aware and shocked that I had been experiencing God's absence for two years. Perhaps beginning to recognize the true extent of the depths into which I had spun, I turned to the concept of lament as expressed beautifully and richly by Michael Card in his book, *A Sacred Sorrow*. I had spent some time with the Psalms, with Job and with Jeremiah prior to reading this book, aware of receiving some little comfort in knowing that I wasn't alone in my experience. However, coming to a deeper understanding of lament, of directly engaging with suffering and its consequences for our relationship with God and building up a more comprehensive picture of the Bible's discourse on grief expressed helped me to begin the process of accepting my situation as it was. This was only a first, very tentative step, but it was a turning from a constant pushing and straining against reality—that continuous cycling between rage and despair—to a recognition that my experience, my pain, might have something to teach me.

Throughout the entire duration of this experienced absence of God, I had made various attempts at the form of contemplative prayer I had discovered in Ilkley, on some occasions even managing to commit to regular sessions over short periods of time. Usually, the experience would leave me disheartened and I would not be able to sustain a commitment to it for very long. During one of these attempts, one day in May of 2015, I quickly recognized my struggle to settle into the discipline, and fell instead into a conversation with God that was built to some extent on my reading about lament. I found myself to be in a mood similar to Jacob at his belligerent moment, and I figuratively stomped up to God and demanded a fight. I wanted to have it out, take the blows, make my demands, remind God of those New Testament promises (ask and you will receive . . .). I had asked and asked, and had never had a reply. And I wasn't asking for a Ferrari, a lottery win or a new house—I was asking for the thing I firmly believed God wanted for me above anything else: companionship with him. So why wouldn't he help me break whatever barrier was between us and restore the friendship and intimacy that we used to know?

I'm still not sure whether that prayer played a key part in the progress of my experience of God's absence, but it was one that stuck very firmly in my memory, containing strong visual as well as spoken elements. It didn't feel as though God responded in any way, but I did feel there was some relief in allowing myself to become angry, as opposed to my usual subserviently contorted approach. Perhaps the fault *was* all mine, but unless God would show me how, I wasn't going to expend any more effort on trying to turn myself into what he wanted me to be!

It was around the time of that prayer that I began to recognize what I believed to be a further consequence of experiencing God's absence. And it was simply that my soul no longer seemed able to connect with beauty in any way that it had formerly done. Stunning landscapes and seascapes; heart-lifting music; a freshly-tidied flower-bed; a river running through woodland; none of it had the capacity to capture and delight me in the way it previously had. At times, I even struggled to engage meaningfully with my own husband and children, relying on habit and function to sustain those central relationships in my life. The most appropriate word I could find to describe the experience was *death*. I might have been living, but it was largely a mechanical existence.

From there, I finally got around to doing something I had known I ought to do for a long while: I booked a retreat. I decided to go to Ampleforth Abbey in North Yorkshire, somewhere I hadn't been before. By then I found it difficult to believe that anything could be said or done that would be any use or remedy. In stark contrast to previous retreat experiences, I approached it with deep reluctance, and because I felt myself to be at a loss to make sense of my spiritual state, I arranged to meet with one of the monks for at least one session.

Chapter 5

Letting go

It was a struggle, but eventually
I gave it all up. Everything.
I thought it would be like
letting go of a rope dangling
down over a dark chasm:
a sudden crash to a stone floor,
then pain and loss from a goodbye
that ripped open my old worldview
and spilled it like vomit
into the black hole
that is you.
But instead the chasm, the rope,
the letting go—it's all disappeared
completely
as if it had never been.
And where you once were is now
blank, as though you had voided
the centre of my world.
You'd think I would be spinning off
into the incoherent distance
but you have committed the perfect crime:
removing not only yourself from the scene,
but any evidence in me
that you were once here.
You have excised my emotions,
my capacity to comprehend,

and my curiosity, as though
what was once my deepest love
has dwindled to a single speck of dust
for me to flick away.

As retreats usually do when approached in a sensible way, this one created the space that I needed. I was able to examine my personal roadblock through a combination of long walks, journaling and discussions with my spiritual advisor.

I already knew that I was hemmed within a narrow, dank and dark avenue; it felt as though I was being led even deeper down that path, as my reflections exposed the intensity of the emotions and the arguments and the emptiness of my soul, bestowing on me a far fuller awareness of the utter blackness within which I was contained. I gained a new understanding of how completely I had lost any sense of being able to discern God's wishes; how thoroughly my ability to trust God had vanished; and how gut-achingly lonely I had become. By this point I felt as though there was nothing left that God could take away from me that could be a possible point of connection with him. Following the aforementioned spiritual losses of the previous year, it seemed as though every pillar that I had relied upon to steady the crumbling edifice of my relationship with him had been destroyed. It was no doubt a great advantage that I didn't know what would be in store for me the following year.

As it was, however, I felt I could go no lower than I already was, and I knew I had never been that low before. Even when living in Belfast, experiencing the first great struggle of my faith, I had not faced such spiritual devastation. I had no idea how to bear the confusion and sorrow and longing, no-one who I felt was able to share the burden with me. Richard had always been that person, but was experiencing his own stresses and difficulties in handling his first incumbency, and for the first time in our marriage I had begun hesitating to share much of my pain with him.

It was in that context that the deepest, most fundamental questions confronted me whilst on retreat at Ampleforth. Firstly: did God love me any more? Did he really, at his core, want me to be part of his life? And secondly: did I want to continue living as though God was part of my life?

Let me try and clarify how extremely difficult it was to even allow that last question space in my thoughts. In eighteen years of faith, I had never experienced the slightest doubt of God's existence. For most of that time I had known that God loved me fully and deeply. My belief in him hadn't dissipated, and so to ask that question was to face the prospect of consciously turning away from a being who, in my understanding, was the very centre of the universe, and who was (or ought to be) love personified. The pain it caused me to ask that question—and I can still remember exactly where I was when I asked it, the memory has seared itself so clearly in my mind—was as though all my previous pain had been concentrated a hundredfold. Yet I still gave it serious thought, and I believe that it was because I recognized the importance of the question that I was able to answer it at least with faith, if still devoid of hope and love. Something in me held on, and wouldn't let me turn away, no matter how dark and desperate things had become.

It was meeting with my spiritual adviser that gave me the beginnings of an answer to the second question, of whether God loved me. I poured out my story, sometimes with great difficulty, but anxious to convey a complete context for my current state of emptiness. My need for Father Christopher to understand and empathize with my experience was intense, and I was aware I was potentially setting myself up for a terrible disappointment if I failed to express myself clearly. The corresponding relief, then, when he accepted my story—seemed to understand the weight I was experiencing—was immense. We had some time for discussion, and I was hoping for that one illuminating moment, a flashlight of understanding so that I would know the way forward, though I knew it was a hope unlikely to be fulfilled. I knew because the darkness over my understanding was too heavy and intense to lift so suddenly. However, Father Christopher was able to recommend some reading material for me that struck me simply by the nature of its title: *The Way of Paradox*, a title by Cyprian Smith, which serves extremely well as an introduction to the works of Meister Eckhart.[4]

What caught my attention first of all was the title. Containing the word "paradox", it pointed towards something I had long held to be an important part of my faith: the apparent contradictions that one has to live with in order to exist within the kingdom of God. Someone who embraced this aspect of faith, I reasoned, was likely to have further profound ideas to challenge and stretch me. Secondly, Father Christopher described Eckhart's understanding of the spiritual journey in a way that intrigued me. Spiritual growth, as I had experienced it to that point, had relied on taking small, incremental steps in understanding and allowing various spiritual truths to take root in my life. I had assumed that this slow, steady progress would continue to increase my ability to submit myself to God's love, eventually leading to . . . who knows what sort of union? Eckhart, Father Christopher explained, followed a path that, rather than taking this sort of circuitous, steady route to that deepest level of knowing God, drove directly towards him, to the "pure essence of consciousness which is the image of God in us" as Cyprian Smith describes it in *The Way of Paradox*. This concept thrilled me, and I borrowed Father Christopher's copy of the book whilst at Ampleforth, devouring the entire text within a day and a half.

Needless to say, although Cyprian Smith does an excellent job of distilling Eckhart's thinking and teaching, it was a conceptually challenging read, and I fully confess that I probably understood less than half of the book's content. However, I did not need reams of fresh understanding to feed hope: I simply needed to recognize that there was a different way of looking at the spiritual journey and a different way of understanding God, that Eckhart could help me to find. If I could not make another small, incremental step towards understanding God and who I was in him, I could choose instead to forsake the winding path and forge one that headed directly to him. I didn't know how, yet, but I knew it was possible. That simple recognition led me to something I had lacked for what felt like an immensely long time: it led me to hope.

I didn't leave Ampleforth with a gift bag of answers, but I had, after all, addressed an incredibly painful question and found a path that was worth exploring. It felt as though I had turned a corner, or even reversed direction completely. Yes, I was still achingly exhausted and in pain at God's absence, but there was a tiny flicker at the core of my soul, a faint light that I was determined to nurture until it was able to illuminate where God was and how I could return to him.

◆   ◆   ◆

By the end of the summer of 2015, still with the sense that the bleakest experience of despair was behind me, I began to look for a new spiritual director. I had to that point been informally meeting with a fellow member of the spirituality team I was a part of, and received firm encouragement from her to look further afield, given that there were few spiritual directors in our area at the time. I didn't have much faith in the possibility of finding someone who would be able to understand and engage with the situation I felt myself to be in, but nevertheless I began my enquiries.

It was also around this time that I began to feel a stronger sense that there was some "thing" that was coming in between God and me. I was hard put to express it any more clearly than that, and on reflection it now sounds like nothing more than an echo of the circular conversations I had been having with myself since 2013 along the lines of:

"Something has caused this separation—"

"It can't be God . . . why would he do that to me . . . ?"

"It must be me—"

"If it was me, I would have some sense of what I'd done—"

"I haven't done anything to cause this, it's something else—"

"What can have caused this separation . . . ?"

. . . and so on, and so on. However, this thought-cycle had somehow become interrupted, creating an opening for new idea-seeds to fall.

Where my thoughts took me at that point was a no less difficult place. I might even say that the darkness became a little thicker again. Because I found myself beginning to suspect that *acquiring* or *achieving* some level or gift or understanding was not the way forward after all. I began instead to give space to the idea of "letting go". Despite everything I felt I had already lost, and the loneliness and isolation I had been left with, it had begun to feel there was more to lose—but that at this point, my own will had to be complicit in the process.

Given how uncertain I was about my own thoughts (and had been for quite some time by now) it was impossible to be sure if any of my ideas were right; if I was really following a route God wanted me to take. I was unable to anchor any of my interpretations of what was happening to me to a particular worldview or theological understanding. My entire sense of what was true and right and of God by this point had crumbled to dust in the dark. I was scrabbling at invisible walls trying to find any opening that made sense, or half-sense—or even no sense, if that was what it took. But if I could make out even the slightest outline of a fissure in this darkness, it was the possibility that God was asking me if I could give up—not him, but the blessings that are usually a natural consequence of intimacy with him, such as connection, closeness, conversation and home. I think it's possible that he was asking, ultimately: "If all the gifts I have ever given you were taken away, would you still remain with me?"

◆   ◆   ◆

In the early spring of 2016 I found a new spiritual director, and despite my screaming anxieties that all my hopes would be balled up like an old piece of newspaper and stuffed under the sofa, it turned out, after all, to be someone who could connect with and ask astute questions about my experiences and thought processes. It's very difficult to express the relief I felt about this. It was perhaps the first time in three years that I felt as though I wasn't being actively pushed away; that a tiny morsel had been offered that enabled me to progress. I didn't hold back during that first session, as I wanted to be clear that my new spiritual director could handle the complexity and intensity of my experience. She listened to it all with a grace and generosity that I remain thankful for, to both her and God, whose gift she brought to me.

There was a cost attached to the opportunity to be vulnerable, however. It was as though suddenly having someone who could grasp what I was trying to express threw into sharp relief how difficult the previous months and years had been. That same month I struggled with feeling, if anything, more vulnerable and lost than ever. I became so much more clearly aware of how alone I had been in my experience. While there were a few people with whom I had tried to discuss what was happening to me, none had been able to identify with my story on a sufficient level to understand and empathize. It was as though I had been a stick that was being whittled away at both ends; so many things that were part of my identity being stripped off at one end, and at the other, the ability to share the experience with others. I was left with the feeling that there was almost nothing of me left. My journal entries from the time touch on the despair I felt: and I do not use that word lightly. It is not a throwaway term to describe some transitory sorrow or heaviness. It is the horrifying sense that there is no purpose or meaning in anything, that there never will be, and that God, who once filled your whole world with light and sustenance and a sense of being complete, would never come back.

The light of being listened to therefore served to illuminate how heavy and painful my struggles had become, and this led to an increase in the resentment I felt towards God. If he was truly with me, all it would take would be some small indication that everything would be all right; why couldn't he give me that? I ached with the need to know that we would be together again, that he loved me, that he wanted me.

Then there was an evening when I was in the garden, not long after my meeting with my new spiritual director. Night had fallen, and the stars were faint but present, as I let the dog out for her bedtime excursion. I stood looking at the sky for a little while, and found myself praying. It felt no different to what I had become used to, my words bouncing off infinity and coming back to me without finding a home, restless now that they were spoken and taunting my mind and spirit as they hovered, unreceived by anyone. Still, it was the first time that I was able to understand at more than a superficial, intellectual level, a truth that I had been trying to persuade myself of for a very long time: that God was with me no matter how little it seemed to be true.

There comes a point, I think, when we engage in the journey of growing closer to God, that certain thoughts or ideas become knowledge on a much more profound level than an academic or scientist could ever describe: as though a gong is struck deep within our souls and fills every inch of us with a new understanding of a long-known truth. These to me feel like immensely fertile points in spiritual growth, when the promise of transformation becomes much more than a possibility, but something we are living to our fullest potential.

That moment of prayer, although having no instant effect on how I felt about myself, the world or God, marked a gradual but significant change in the trajectory of my thoughts and hopes. New, if faint possibilities began to open up in the ongoing interactions (if such they could be called) between God and me.

One experience I had shortly after that prayer struck me strongly enough to note it down in my journal. I had bought a new album from a folk duo that Richard and I love. It happened that I was listening to the album whilst driving somewhere in the car, and one particular song came on. I had listened to it before, but this time, something was different. This time it suddenly felt as though God was using the words as an invitation to me. They go something like this:

> Wanted to bring you a brand new story
> Wanted to sing you a brand new song
> Hoping the notes would flow real easy
> Hoping the words wouldn't take too long
> I didn't want to make you think
> I didn't want to make you frown
> But in the heart of a quiet little English town
> Walk with me when the sun goes down.[5]

The experience was so strong, the sense so clear, that I was reduced to tears as I listened. Subsequent listenings had a similar effect, and sometimes do even now.

It's difficult, at this point, to track the way my thoughts and experiences developed and changed—the connections between each of the events that have led me to where I am now—but I think that receiving such a beautifully generous and welcoming invitation had a key part to play in instigating the next significant experience I had in prayer, which came near the end of that March.

Chapter 6

You

You are not who I thought
I needed you to be.
I have stumbled into thick fog,
and cannot tell whether
it is the sun or moon that rises;
the grey air shrouds my eyes.
But you are the fog, and
you are the panic in my blindness.
You are the sun, and the moon.
You are the monochrome sky
under which I walk
and you are the slamming
of the door to my soul.
You are every scream of my heart
that disappears into the muffled landscape;
you are the nothingness
I find myself to be
since, at your bidding,
I parted from the you I used to know.
You are everything I have lost
and everything that I must not
expect to gain.
But I will hold myself here,
within the grey sky,
since I would rather see that I am blind
than be blind to what I cannot see.

In my thoughts I have begun to refer to this experience as my "prayer of acceptance". I remember that I sat down purposefully to pray, as I thought I should try contemplative prayer. However, I was so out of the habit, and my head was so full of thoughts and feelings, that I set that plan aside after a short attempt. I little wanted to engage in another one-sided conversation, but my words seemed the only way forward at that point, and so I began expressing my thoughts in the hope that God would break his usual habit of silence. Despite my recognition that his presence was assured, and despite his abundantly generous invitation within the words of *Walk with me*, I was still uncertain of his desire for me.

And so we spoke. And it did truly feel as though, for the first time in years, God was near to me, hearing my words, receiving my emotions. And it truly felt as though he responded to me, offering wisdom and insight. It was as though, having been locked in a box devoid of light and air, a small window had opened and I was beginning to be able to breathe again.

We came to an extremely important place during that conversation. I believe it to have been one of the most significant experiences in my faith journey so far, and that its effects will continue to be felt for a long time to come. And yet it was such a simple step to take: all God was asking me to see was that, to this point, my belief in his love for me had always depended on some kind of "experience" of his presence. At this stage, I find it extremely difficult to describe that experience, apart from to say that I never remember its absence from the time I first spoke to him in my mother's kitchen. Perhaps it is best described as being "filled up" with knowing that he was with me. During that conversation I began to question why that had always been the case for me—was my faith really so weak that God had felt this "feeling" was the only way he could ensure that it would endure? Perhaps it was.

Now, though, I realized that God was asking me to take a step forward that was at once infinitesimal and almost insurmountable. He invited me to try trusting him without that safeguard in place. I can put it no other way. There was no pressure, no demand; simply the opening up of a new possibility, and the space and freedom for me to consider whether it was something I could do.

Having become so clearly aware of my failures of faith and trust to that point, where else could I go, then, but to the place I had always previously felt was the safest of all? Of course I said yes to God; of course it was enough to know without experiencing; of course I wanted him to make my faith stronger. I won't deny it was difficult, because I knew that in theory I was committing to never having any "experience" of God this side of eternity, but I had become very clear in my own mind that God, after all, was more important than my own experience of him. That I belonged to him no matter what. That I was ready to be tested and show myself better able to trust him. And, ultimately, that no matter how I "felt", the fullness of his presence would always be there, making itself known in ways so deep I may not even be able to recognize them.

◆   ◆   ◆

One might expect such a pivotal point in a person's faith journey to liberate them fully and immediately from any prison of their own making. However, I was still locked in that box, even though the window was open and the fresh air continued, occasionally, to feed me with hope. I still habitually struggled with the sense that God wasn't listening, and with resentment and anger that he had chosen such a time as Margaret's death to begin this process. However, those things were ever so slowly beginning to loosen their hold on me by this point, though I was very aware that it would take time and patience to reach a state of peace. I was relieved to have some tools to hand, now, to help me get there. I was ready to do the work involved, but was still emotionally and spiritually very fragile.

One of the first outward signs that the faintest breeze was beginning to stir and shift the heavy fog of my anger and resentment came the following month: I went to a concert to see a favourite band—in fact, the band whose song had briefly stirred me not long before. It was a very long time since I had heard any live music, and being very used by this point to the constant feeling of "deadness" that ordinarily left me feeling disconnected from what was going on around me, I was startled to realize that something in me had begun to wake up. The music wasn't just notes and singing; it was alive, and it stirred life in me. I welcomed the experience, delighted in it, and longed for the time when I would be fully awake, fully alive and revelling in the gifts of God once more.

It was over the next two months that the idea began to solidify that had been on my mind since the middle of the previous year. It felt as though God was asking me to let go. I still didn't know what, or why, or what purpose it might fulfil, or even how to do it, but it began to make sense. I had struggled for so long with questions about who God was and who I was, which lent such an air of unreality to everything else beyond, that perhaps it was my need to have answers that I needed to let go of; and maybe, in that letting go, everything else was contained.

Perhaps this awareness developed in me because I had by that point recognized my own culpability in the severing of my relationship with God. Perhaps God felt I was strong enough at that point to be able to say, "Everything I have known, I renounce." Because doing that is a terrifying prospect. At least when I had my anger and resentment to cling on to, I had a connection to the past, with what I had once known to be true. Letting go of those things leaves a person with nothing, no way of understanding God, or the world, or their place in it. Letting go meant accepting, finally, that I had to go forward from that point, and not hide in the limitations of my former truth. It was another call to faith, and I struggled a great deal, cursing my own weakness, but eventually submitted despite my fear.

The place where this process left me is best encapsulated in these lines from the poem that heads this chapter:

> I have stumbled into thick fog,
> and cannot tell whether
> it is the sun or moon that rises;
> the grey air shrouds my eyes.

I believe it was another important step to take, following that prayer of acceptance. Still not an easy place to be, but the conclusion to the poem indicates a change in my mood and my ability to accept the unknown:

> since I would rather see that I am blind
> than be blind to what I cannot see.

In hindsight, it looks as though these movements forward were preparations God was making in me for the retreat that I had booked for June that year.

◆　　◆　　◆

I entered my retreat of 2016 without any particular expectation as to what benefits might arise from it. I went more out of a sense of obedience, knowing the wisdom of taking some time each year away from the intensity of everyday life to seek God. I was exhausted, physically, emotionally and spiritually. Compared to the previous year's retreat, which I had entered into in an agitated and desperate state, this time I simply wanted to stop. Life carries on no matter what spiritual movements might be happening to a person internally, and with a husband in ministry and three children, the pace can sometimes feel relentless. It felt like a blessing, at least, to find quietness and solitude.

A second blessing I received during those few days was a sense that the "grey air" was ever so slowly beginning to lighten a little more. The breeze that had so lightly begun to stir that thick fog at the Show of Hands concert continued to do its work. I still felt unable to see, but somehow the pressure, or weight, had lifted slightly. A shift, perhaps, from despair towards some centre ground between that suffocating darkness and the fresh air of hope that might once again infuse me in the future.

Having chosen a rural location for my retreat, I spent a great deal of time walking, and in my times of rest I either wrote or read. I came across a book on contemplative prayer that I hadn't previously read and decided to see if it could shed any light on the difficulties I was having with it. I had never lost the sense that contemplative, silent prayer was something of a "prayer-home" to me, and I felt drawn to discovering more about it if I could. Reading about it again stirred me, and I felt that now might be an appropriate time to begin again, this time with a regular, daily commitment. Quite how I was to manage that around family responsibilities I hadn't worked out, other than getting up even earlier in the morning, but I knew it was something I had to work out.

The last significant event during that retreat was one day near the end, when I revisited the question I had asked myself on retreat the previous year: "Do I want to walk away from God?" What I found in the asking was that the question itself had lost its power. I had, at the very least, ceased to think of the possibility that God and I might never meet again.

Again, I had taken a step forward. Though still locked in the box, the weight of loss still pressing down on me, I felt as though even if I didn't have the key, it had become that bit more possible that I would discover it. I tried very hard not to be impatient, not to demand the key from God, but to learn patience and submission—though I think perhaps I didn't try hard enough. I was bone-weary, spiritually aching and lonely, and so very desperate for the bleakness to end. For a short while after this retreat I felt quite positive, but it wasn't many weeks before I slipped into resentment and anger again. I suppose I was still, even then, looking back and longing for what had been, no matter how often I told myself that the only way out of the loneliness was through anticipating something new.

◆   ◆   ◆

Recovery is slow

Grief enters the ring
like a 300lb pro,
parries your every featherweight jab
and with one neatly placed
uppercut spreads you out
on the floor, your body bruised
from scalp to toe.
But there's no whistle-blow,
no referee to call time:
instead, Grief hangs on,
pins you to the floor and stabs
at every wound until he finds a way
to get beneath your skin.
You may bleed, but no-one
tries to stem the flow.
Instead the surgeon, armed with
ice-sharp tools,
excises your capacity to feel,
and stuffs the cavity with grey dust
so that when you wake up you won't know
how deeply Grief has burrowed in.
When you rise, the dust will
sift away, but don't kid yourself—
recovery is slow.

The next part of the journey is, I think, the most difficult to convey. It involves sharing the vulnerabilities of another person, who was graciously kind enough to allow me to divulge his story.

You could say a fuse had been lit beneath our house when Margaret died. It was a long fuse, because it took a full three years for it to ignite the bomb we should have known would explode sooner or later. Richard, who had either not been given or not given himself enough time to grieve, had begun to drive himself too deeply into his work, and everything else he may have felt had become buried beneath a wall of anger. We had been functioning as a family, but in August 2016 I—perhaps simply a little more able to look around me and notice what was happening—began to get worried. I could no longer appease myself by thinking, "His stress is only short term; he'll soon be able to relax", because even when the opportunities came there was no relaxation to be found, for either of us. His emotional numbness had begun to affect not just his work, but our family life. Little things happened that caused me to question the strength and resilience of our relationship, which was something I had never questioned in our seventeen years together.

I resolved, then, to find some time to talk about what was happening. I wanted to express how troubled I was about our relationship, but needed time and space and peace to do so. It cost me some sadness, but the only opportunity I could find was when we took a short anniversary break away from the children. No-one wants to spend their anniversary talking about the problems in their relationship, but I was worried enough that I was ready to sacrifice relaxation for the sake of our marriage. However, it didn't surprise me that Richard resisted the discussion at first, and was left shaken and troubled once we had talked.

Of even greater difficulty was that almost immediately after our anniversary break, we were to travel to Northern Ireland with the children to visit Richard's family. It was our first visit in two years, and I knew Richard was anxious as to how he would be able to handle being physically closer to the reality of his mother's death.

We were both so tired and ragged that we were desperate for a good holiday, one that would give us space to wind down, step away from the daily struggle to keep ourselves afloat, and enjoy a little less responsibility. There was no real way this could be that holiday, though. There were one or two good days, but mostly it was a case of pretending everything was fine and trying not to let our anxieties ruin the children's experience.

When we got home, we began to see the effects of some of the physical and emotional stress that Richard had been experiencing. The most appropriate description for his experience was probably "brown-out". Not quite a breakdown, but something that skated pretty close. He spent most of his days looking grey and sleeping on the sofa when his responsibilities didn't require him to be active. He would make an enormous effort to drag himself to church services and any other events he was committed to, and simply fade out in between.

We discussed some of the options for professional support that he might seek, and the fact that he was able to consider those possibilities gave me some hope. However, by the end of that August we were very aware of the looming autumn term, which was extremely full of work that had been organized before his illness had come to a head. I dreaded it, on my own behalf as well as his; I can't even begin to imagine how he managed to face up to the challenge.

September was therefore spent taking one day at a time, watching for signs of unrecoverable exhaustion or stress, on a knife-edge of tension. It helped him come to a decision though, and he accepted his need for help to understand his illness and begin recovering from it.

I'm not sure I can pinpoint the time at which I began to realize the cost that having a partner close to mental breakdown demanded of me. My first response had been very practical: I had recognized his need for rest during those August weeks, though I wasn't even sure it was rest—perhaps it was simply his body acknowledging how far over its limits he had been pushing it. I had taken up the slack, stepping in to take up some of his usual responsibilities in the house, managing most of the children's issues and concerns, dealing with back-to-school arrangements. It was as though my emotional response had shut down at that point, as I was very aware that I was experiencing no feelings in reaction to the situation at all; all I could do was ensure the household continued to run as best as possible.

I think that it was actually at a point not long after Richard accepted his need for professional help that I began to experience the physical and emotional effects of my own stress and anxiety. Perhaps it was something to do with feeling as though a part of the burden had been lifted that caused me to start becoming more self-aware again. Tension had left my body sore and aching; feeling bereft of the one person who I had always trusted to be there for me left my heart lonelier and more broken than ever. I could see quite clearly how our lives had come to this point: it all made sense in retrospect, from one step to the next, but how I wept. I was desolate, without God, my husband unable to offer comfort, with insufficient strength to carry my own pain, let alone be the wife or mother I knew I ought to be.

I am not sure how I made it through the months leading up to that Christmas. Always a busy term, it exacts high demands in terms of Richard's work and the children's school commitments, and at that time I was also trying to build up a new business in editorial work. If I'm honest, that was the only thing I had any enthusiasm for. It gave me something to focus on outside of the horror-show in my own mind and soul. I had the opportunity to spend time in other people's worlds, which was a welcome distraction, and by that December I had progressed well enough to begin securing work that I enjoyed as much for the content as for being able to utilize my proofreading and copy-editing skills.

Strangely enough, this was also a period in which I reinstated my practice of contemplative prayer. Given that it meant rising half an hour earlier than usual, this took some extra toll on my energy, yet I was particularly drawn to practising it. I am sure now that God was actively working in my efforts to connect with him, though I could not see any direct benefits at the time, and I may never fully understand why I was able to make such a commitment at such a difficult time.

The Christmas holidays were to be my respite. There would of course be hosting and entertaining to do, but there would also be two weeks of reduced demands on my time, more relaxed mornings, more opportunities to restore my physical energy. So I watched as Richard put in place coping strategies to help him both manage and work through his illness, and waited as patiently as I could for the rest I knew I needed.

◆   ◆   ◆

I felt unusually tired during the first week of the holidays. My first diagnosis was that it was a physical reaction to the emotional intensity and pressure of the previous few months. Since I had never experienced such high levels of stress before, I had no way of knowing how my body would react when some of the responsibility let up and I was able to rest. And it may have been a part of the problem. However, after almost a week, I realized that the lack of energy I continued to feel had strong similarities to the effects of viruses I had suffered from in the past. Cross with myself for not recognizing the symptoms sooner, I prescribed myself some proper rest. That helped to some degree, but the tiredness and unwell feeling clung on throughout the entire holiday, and I was left feeling physically worse at the end than I felt at the beginning. The rest that I had longed for and believed so strongly that I desperately needed had completely eluded me.

In the time when I had known God was near to me I may have questioned that experience more energetically. How could there be no room for me to breathe at a time when I so clearly needed it? Couldn't he have protected me, just a little, where I was unable to protect myself? Just how abandoned and discarded did I have to feel before he would allow his aloof gaze to fall back on me and give me some infinitesimal indication that he actually did love me after all?

However, I suppose I had become used, in some ways, to my life being separate from God. Certainly the part of me that would have previously felt wounded was simply numb, and those questions slipped into the void that had already stolen all my questions and rage and loneliness.

◆　　◆　　◆

It was a surprise, therefore, that during the first few weeks of 2017 I began to experience tiny moments of what I can only describe as "awakening". An odd scrap of poetry would form itself in my mind, then dissipate after a brief moment. A strange sensation would sometimes occur if I heard or saw something beautiful. It took a couple of these occasions to recognize feelings that, before God's absence, I had been very used to experiencing. Now, feeling that spark again, the best way I could describe it was like glimpses of resurrection.

As I say, these moments were tiny and fleeting, and then towards the end of January I injured my back. That clouded the following two months with terrible pain, followed by slow easing, followed by more injury, and so the cycle continued until the day Daniel had an accident at school and needed to go to hospital to find out whether his leg was broken. I was the parent available, so I went with him, and though the experience was by no means as awful as it could have been, by the end of it the pain in my back was like the fires of Mordor.[6] That was enough to send me stumbling to the doctor, who prescribed strong medication and a better attempt at balancing work and rest.

The whole scenario meant that on top of the tiredness produced by stress, I was also exhausted from living in continuous pain of varying levels. I was therefore struggling to sustain my commitment to a regular habit of contemplative prayer, though it continued to be my favoured method for approaching God. After the first "awakening" experiences of the new year, I fell back into knowing only the grey fog that had dogged me for so long, and allowed resentment and bitterness to take a stronger hold again. I wanted to be out of that fog so very badly.

My back began to recover by the end of March, and as the year crept into April and the pain cleared, I began to get a better sense of the extent of my own stress and emotional exhaustion. In the months since Christmas Richard had been taking great care to implement strategies to help himself, and was showing early but good signs of recovery. At that point I had hoped I would start to see signs within myself of improved emotional health. However, the strength of my need for God, and the aching chasm between us, were no less. No doubt it was the combination of the spiritual and emotional stress together that left me feeling so weary.

Holy Week came, and the story of Mary Magdalene's reunion with Jesus after his resurrection strayed across my path again, eliciting the most visceral reaction to it that I have ever experienced. Sitting in church and listening to the reading, I felt a sudden, desperate need for Jesus to say my name in the way he had said hers. Then my eyes, too, would be opened, and I could see him in a new light; one short step and our relationship would be restored.

The experience didn't leave me, and the following week when we were holidaying in Scotland, I felt a strong urge to explore Mary's story in imaginative prayer. Being little-practised at such prayer and not in a place of confidence or strength, I found the imagination part difficult, but did find I was able to have some sort of exchange with Jesus that showed me more about myself, even if it didn't bring me any nearer to a sense of God's love for me. It was the starting point of recognizing my own anger, which I had known of in theory to that point but had not actually felt to any great extent; it also freed me to honestly admit that my ability to judge what might be needed to "fix" my relationship with God was completely malfunctioning. I had been so used to being able to trust my instincts and intuition, and finally, at this point, I began to recognize and accept that this was no longer possible. In my journal at the time I wrote: "I feel as though I am missing something that is at once incredibly simple and yet deeply profound." There was a helplessness to the admission at the time, but at least it laid the first stones of a new pathway towards God.

I discussed my response to Mary's story with my spiritual director in our following session, and digging deeper into that reaction drew even greater pain from me, as if lancing a wound. Musing over the session in my journal a few days later, I began to consider the tension between my promise to God, that I would be his whether I could sense his presence or not, and the prevailing sensing of "deadness" I was experiencing, while being aware that emotion is usually a part of any healthy relationship. It did seem likely at that point that something was blocking us from each other, and that that something was likely to be my own anger. Whether anger at the manner of Margaret's death, or at God's apparent abandonment of me when I had needed him so desperately, I didn't know.

During that spiritual direction session, I agreed with my director that it was time to stop contemplative prayer for a while. Despite having made some progress in my understanding of what was happening to me, which could have been attributed to the continued discipline, it felt more important to permit myself a rest from the strenuous routine. Pragmatically, I had known for some while that the cost had been greater than any benefit, and though the decision was made difficult by my desperation to find a way out of the spiritual fog, it was a liberation for my body, which delighted in the benefits of extra sleep.

It wasn't many weeks then until my next retreat, which I looked forward to with a kind of awful anticipation, desperate for something to happen to break the wretched impasse I continued to find myself to be in, yet fearful that there would be little to hope for. Resentment and bitterness continued to visit me, and although I didn't slip back into the dreadful despair of previous years, I was once again struggling to find threads of hope to hold on to. I was incredibly grateful, however, that Richard's recovery had continued well enough that he was able to support me to take some time away, as I knew my going would give him extra work in looking after the children. It was a measure of the resilience of our relationship that, though he had quite rightly needed to focus quite sharply on enabling his return to health, he was able to recognize and help to fulfil my need for spiritual inquiry and solace.

For my retreat of 2017 I had chosen St Anthony's Priory, where I had originally discovered my call to spiritual direction and where I had trained to become a spiritual director. It is difficult to describe, even to myself, the mixture of uncertainty, curiosity, longing and anxiety that coloured my decision to go back there. A place that had witnessed and nurtured a significant transition in my spiritual growth, in which my relationship with God had solidified and intensified in a very short space of time, has always been brushed with the flavour of spiritual home for me. And yet since this experience of absence had begun, my connection to it had begun to feel more distant; another cruel consequence, since I had nowhere else I could describe even remotely as a spiritual home by that point. I was therefore completely unprepared for how I would feel about returning, and whether the place that had given me so much help in the past would have anything to offer to me at this juncture.

I was surprised to find myself more at home and comfortable than I had expected. I had elected to have meals provided, which meant joining the community at lunchtimes, where more usually when on retreat I prefer to keep to myself as much as possible. But not having to prepare food gave me more time, and time was what I felt I needed most of all. I spent a great deal of it taking walks, both morning and afternoon, to places both familiar and not. There was still, however, a great deal of time for prayer.

I began with a question that appears in the first chapter of John's Gospel, when Jesus is passing John and his disciples. John points Jesus out to two of his disciples, and they follow Jesus. On turning around and seeing them, Jesus asks: "What do you want?"

I don't know what caused me to return to that question, though it is one I have used to help others explore their relationship with Jesus on many occasions. It had seemed irrelevant to my situation in the recent past, since I was (I thought) fixating on what it was that God wanted. By the end of my first full day I had an answer: I wanted to know whether God loved me. Not in a repeat-a-Bible-verse-verbatim way, or a logical or intellectual way, but in a way that would transform me, and perhaps provide me with the key to unlock the box I was in. A way that would breathe gently on that awful fog I was stuck in, and stir it again. Not only that, but I wanted to receive this knowledge in a way that would not compromise my promise of the previous year: I wanted to be sure that I would not go searching for a spiritual "experience" to reassure myself of God's presence, but that I would give all the power of communication into his hands.

It was helpful to have arrived at a clear answer to that question; to understand the depth of my need to know God's love for me. Alongside those reflections I was also spending time with the idea of emotional blockage. Since I knew that my longing was to be in full fellowship with God, and that longing was taking me nowhere, I was coming to the conclusion that my emotional state since Margaret's death still required a great deal of unpacking. The nature of that blockage still remained a mystery to me, however, since my emotions were not close enough to the surface for me to identify.

The following morning, I spent time praying in the garden, and as my reflections unfolded a word came to me accompanied with a sharp sting and a visceral, physical reaction that immediately caused me to recognize its importance. The word was *fear*. Until that moment I don't think I had realized that I was afraid. Angry, yes. Resentful, definitely. Bitter, most certainly. But afraid? I suddenly realized with great clarity that all these things stemmed, at least in part, from a fear that God didn't love me after all, and that my mistake had been to allow fear to lock me away in my box and stifle my love for and trust in God.

I struggle, usually, with the concept of sin as it is often taught and understood in modern times: I tend to think it is as much a consequence of our choices as a cause. At its root, however, sin conveys the idea of *separation from God*. Notwithstanding how unwittingly I had done it, I had nevertheless allowed sin into my life by entertaining fear and choosing to remain locked away by it. At any moment I had had the freedom to declare, "I choose love; I choose to trust in God."

Later that day, I happened to meet the person who had been my first spiritual director. It was a happy reunion, and we arranged to meet late in the afternoon. I spent most of the day walking, and we caught up over coffee and cake once I returned. It was a real pleasure to chat without the formal structure of a spiritual direction session, so that we could each speak and share information about ourselves. However, I found myself talking a great deal in the end, reviewing the four years since Margaret's death, and one question my companion asked that I found to be a particular challenge was: "Did you have anyone to share these burdens with?"

The answer, of course, was no. There was nobody who knew my spiritual journey from then to now; not even the person to whom I was used to telling everything, the husband who had been trapped in his own prison of depression and stress, and was now expending every effort to ensure his return to health. Not only this, but all the things I had been used to lean on for spiritual support seemed to have been stripped away, one by one. The house move had deprived us of the community that had supported us through the initial period of grieving; I had lost access to the last of the intermediaries between myself and God in 2014; God had already disappeared, and Richard followed a couple of years later; and ultimately I was not even able to find confidence or certainty in myself, since I felt as though everything that I had known to be true about who I was what I knew had been called into question. There was nobody; not even me.

Putting it all together like that, retelling the story and seeing the context for my current situation more clearly, was something of a release. Yes, it filled me with huge sorrow, reflecting later on how thoroughly isolated I had become, and I wept deeply for the situation I found myself to be in, and for my loneliness. However, my companion suggested that I might want to pray imaginatively through the emotional blockage that prevented me from "seeing" God.

It was at that point I realized that I was finally ready to face this blockage head on. I thanked my companion deeply for allowing me to relate at such length what I had been experiencing, and we promised to continue communicating by email after I returned home.

I was determined to attempt this "prayer of unblocking" before the end of the day, no matter how difficult and painful it might become. It took time to find and prepare the physical space that would enable me to prepare internally; this was as much prevarication, I'm sure, as preparation. What if God still had nothing to say to me, and my hope—which had begun to rise since that conversation—was broken once again by silence from the other end?

I began with an attempt to pray imaginatively, as my companion had suggested, but, as with most of my previous attempts at this kind of prayer, it fell by the wayside. My ability to create visual contexts for prayer internally has never been very good, and my need to communicate directly in this case was too urgent: abandoning all attempts to conjure up images through which to connect with God, I spoke instead. It was, quite simply, a prayer of confession; it was the deepest confession I have ever made in my life. I had never at any point before allowed fear to rule me so completely, and its tendrils of resentment, bitterness and anger to suffocate me so thoroughly; and in the naming of these emotions, it felt as though I had only barely begun to understand the strength of their hold on me.

However deeply they had penetrated, and however little I understood at that point, it seemed to be enough for God; that time of prayer, redolent with the sense that he was listening intently, ended in a time of what I could only describe as consolation—a deep, sweet sense of presence, and comfort, and joy. I was amazed, and somewhat hesitant to believe that this was truly God giving me his gift, yet the years of separation seemed to somehow fall away, and he gave me the power to receive what he was ready and eager to give.

The following morning I found myself in the library reading a book by Anthony de Mello. Its title escapes me, but its content led me to meditate on sin, and the place it had taken in my life over the years since Margaret's death. Perceiving my fear as sin, since it had allowed me to experience separation from God, was a start; however, while my prayer of the previous night had been a form of confession, and was the key to unlocking the door of my box, it meant that the sunlight had begun to pour into the crevices of my spirit. Today's task, I began to understand on my morning walk, was to examine in more detail exactly what the light was shining on, and what my responsibilities were following that examination.

Before I returned to the retreat house I had determined that a formal prayer of confession was required, that would address each of the sins that my fear had spawned (which I had identified as resentment, bitterness and anger) as well as the fear itself. I devised a method of prayer that felt particularly appropriate: I drew a picture of each of the four sins, took them one by one, confessing to and repenting of each, then destroying the image as I placed it by a lit candle. It was an unusually formal prayer for me; but then, this was an unusual situation for me to find myself in, and it felt like exactly the right response to the realizations I had come to about myself and my own weakness.

There was no moment of blinding certainty, no dart of pure joy, no physical sense of relief or release; simply a feeling that I had taken the only possible step that could help me out of my loneliness and spiritual isolation from God. Perhaps he could have marked such a momentous event in some way—but then, if he had, I would not have had to exercise my extremely unfit faith muscles to trust in him. An isolated experience of spiritual consolation at that point would, I suspect, have had far less value than the gift that prayer left me with: the realization that I finally felt able to believe that God had my best interests at heart. I was almost taken aback at how quickly following this prayer I realized that I wasn't angry any longer; that resentment and bitterness had faded; and that, more importantly than anything else, I wasn't afraid any more.

Epilogue

I cannot say that the months since that retreat have been marked with certainty, with restoration of self or clarity about who God is. All I know, having come as far as the following April by the end of writing this, is that there is a great deal of healing to accomplish given the wounds that have been inflicted on my spirit over the last few years, and that God appears to be diligently working towards that end.

There was a point in this story at which the best word I could find to describe my experience was *death*. Whilst in it, I could see no way out; I was consigned to an extended period of waiting, which only served to highlight my helplessness and stoke my misguided determination to resist what was happening. I was unable to anticipate any possibility of resurrection then, but while I am still unable to say that I have reached that point yet, I am able to look forward to a time when God will show me what this has all been for.

One thing I am certain of is that the box I had locked myself in for so long is no more. I am, at least for the present, free of fear, and I pray that such a state may continue for a long time to come. I have found an equilibrium, a steadiness that is restorative after so many years of turbulence. I have once again returned to practising contemplative prayer, regularly if less frequently than before, within the limits of what I feel able to manage amongst all the other daily tasks and the confines of my energy levels. I do find a sense of home in it, of belonging, though I have only made small steps so far towards discovering God's silence. I am enduringly grateful to God for his patience towards me for all these years, and for the peace he has enabled me to attain in this waiting time.

For the first time since Margaret's death I actually feel safe. It is still a strange experience to catch myself at odd moments, realizing that I no longer feel that terrible sense of desolation and disconnection. I don't have the answer to the question of why God had to leave me at such a vulnerable point in my life; yet the question no longer has a hold over me. My spirit is anchored, tucked away somewhere I'm not sure even I could find, since any time I press God to find out what I should be doing next, he stops me—quite calmly, but firmly—from going any further right now. It's as though he is saying, "Just wait and rest; I will restore you, and when I am finished, you will understand what you need to understand, and we can build our friendship into something new, that is far deeper than it was before."

And so I continue to wait. However, there is a different texture to my waiting now. Where once I existed in perpetual agitation, I am now at rest. Perhaps it is because I feel that, finally, I have been able to let go fully of what used to be. The relationship between God and me was once one of huge richness, and was delineated within the confines of a relationship between lovers. I am now able to recognize what a blessing it was to me, and at the same time to accept completely that if our relationship is to grow, I need to leave that form of it by the wayside, perhaps in the same way as a snake sheds its skin in order to grow a new one.

I am at peace and content, looking forward to a future of new possibilities with God, and glad to know he is protecting and strengthening me to prepare me for the years to come.

Invisible embrace

I was a clenched fist
gripping tightly around the shape
you used to be,
the emptiness digging sharp nails

into my fingers and palm
till I bled out with loneliness,
grief and fear.
A grace-filled moment flickered past
like an airborne swift,
printing an impression of flight and freedom
in the corner of my eye.
The moment held,
and once-seized knuckle-joints
now felt a pulse, a promise left
within that empty space, that Fear once hid.
Muscles unwound their coiled readiness
for unrelenting pain,
and, within a sacred, head-bowed breath,
released the emptiness
and stretched into an open hand.
The wounds remain;
the scars a story that is only mine to tell.
Yet now, as fresh blood flows
from wrist to finger-tip of me,
I will not dwell on emptiness once held.
Nor can I tell the shape
that holds me now,
suspends me in my narrative
and tends my wounds,
as though the years of separation never were.
And I am bound to wait
for you again; but where my need once raged
to know the form of you and clutch it tight,
I now find rest within the solace
of your cushioning invisibility.

Notes

1   The Elves' safe haven in J. R. R. Tolkien's *The Lord of the Rings*.

2   The director doesn't "direct" in the way we normally understand the word in modern English, but will spend most of the time listening, and, when appropriate, will reflect what they have heard back to the speaker or ask a question to unpack a particular topic in greater detail. For this reason, some practitioners prefer the word "accompaniment" to "direction", as it better indicates the sense of companionship and "travelling with" that are fundamental to the role.

3   A Spanish mystic of the sixteenth century who produced poetry and spiritual writings. He was a member of the Order of Discalced Carmelites and suffered persecution for his loyalty to it. *Dark Night of the Soul* is probably his best-known work. It is an exposition of a poem by the same title that he wrote during a period when he was imprisoned. Both poem and book examine a profound and painful spiritual experience that, despite the apparent devastation it causes in one's soul, nevertheless is a journey towards a much deeper and richer relationship with God.

4   Meister Eckhart was a Christian mystic born in the thirteenth century. He was a member of the Dominican Order, and also a scholar and lecturer, becoming famous during his own lifetime. Near the end of his life he faced controversy over some of the things he taught, and shortly after his death the Pope declared some of his teachings to be heretical. However, the last century or so has seen a renewed interest in his works and a revisiting of some of the ideas that the Church was unable to countenance during his lifetime with fresh perspective.

5   *Walk with me* by Steve Knightley, recorded on the Show of Hands album *The Long Way Home* (2015).

6   I should point out, of course, that Daniel came away from hospital in a far better state than we anticipated: his leg was not broken after all, though still quite sore!